LET'S COLOR
A HOPE STORY

AN INCLUSIVE COLORING BOOK FOR CONFIDENCE AND CARING

SHAWNTA SMITH SAYNER

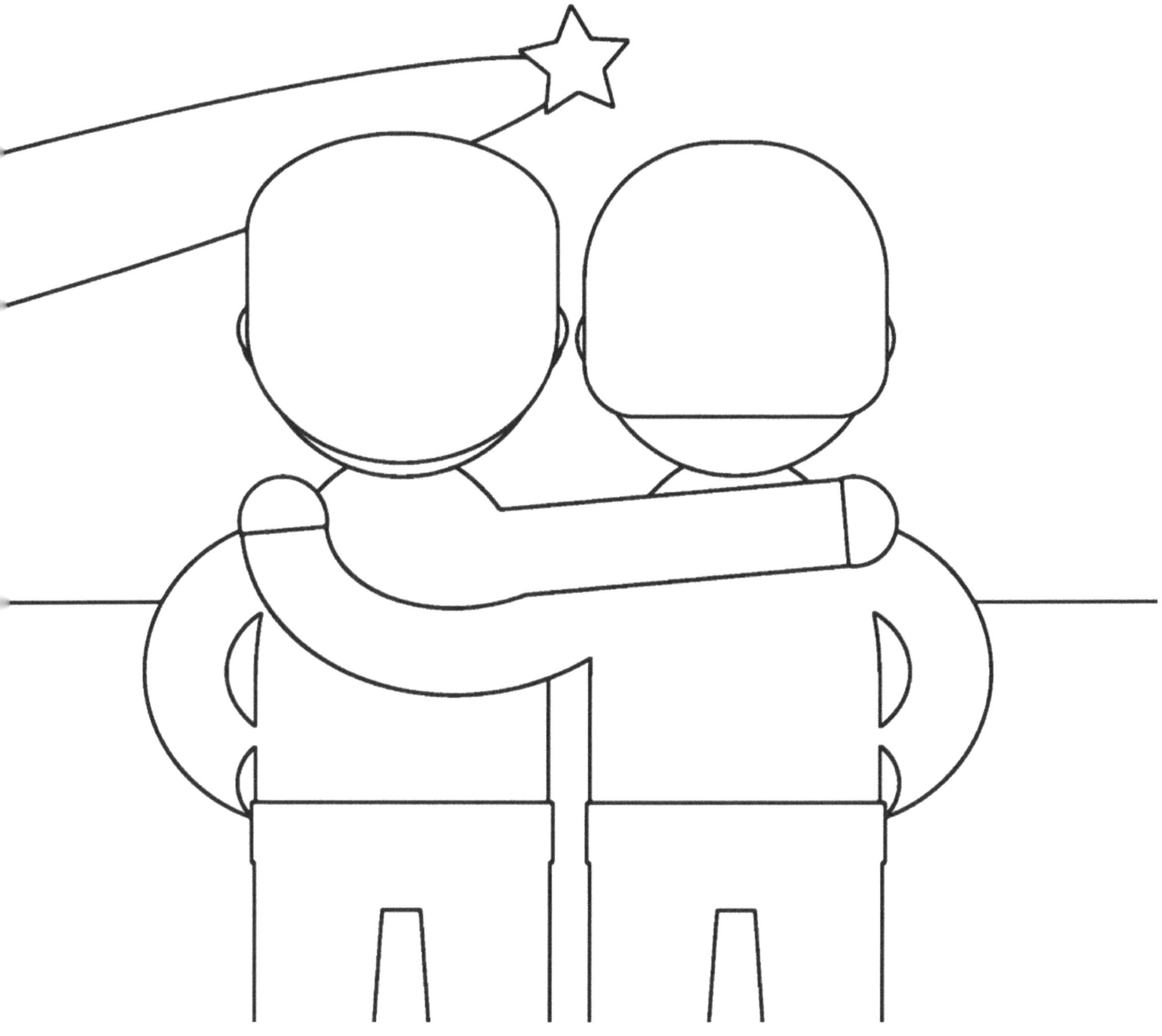

This book is a work of creative nonfiction. Names, characters, places, and incidents are either the product of the author's imagination or are used fictitiously. Any resemblance to actual persons, living or dead, business establishments, events, or locales is entirely coincidental.

Library of Congress Cataloging-in-Publication Data available
Library of Congress Control Number: 2021909046
ISBN: 978-1-952944-14-7

First Edition: May 2021

THIS BOOK BELONGS TO

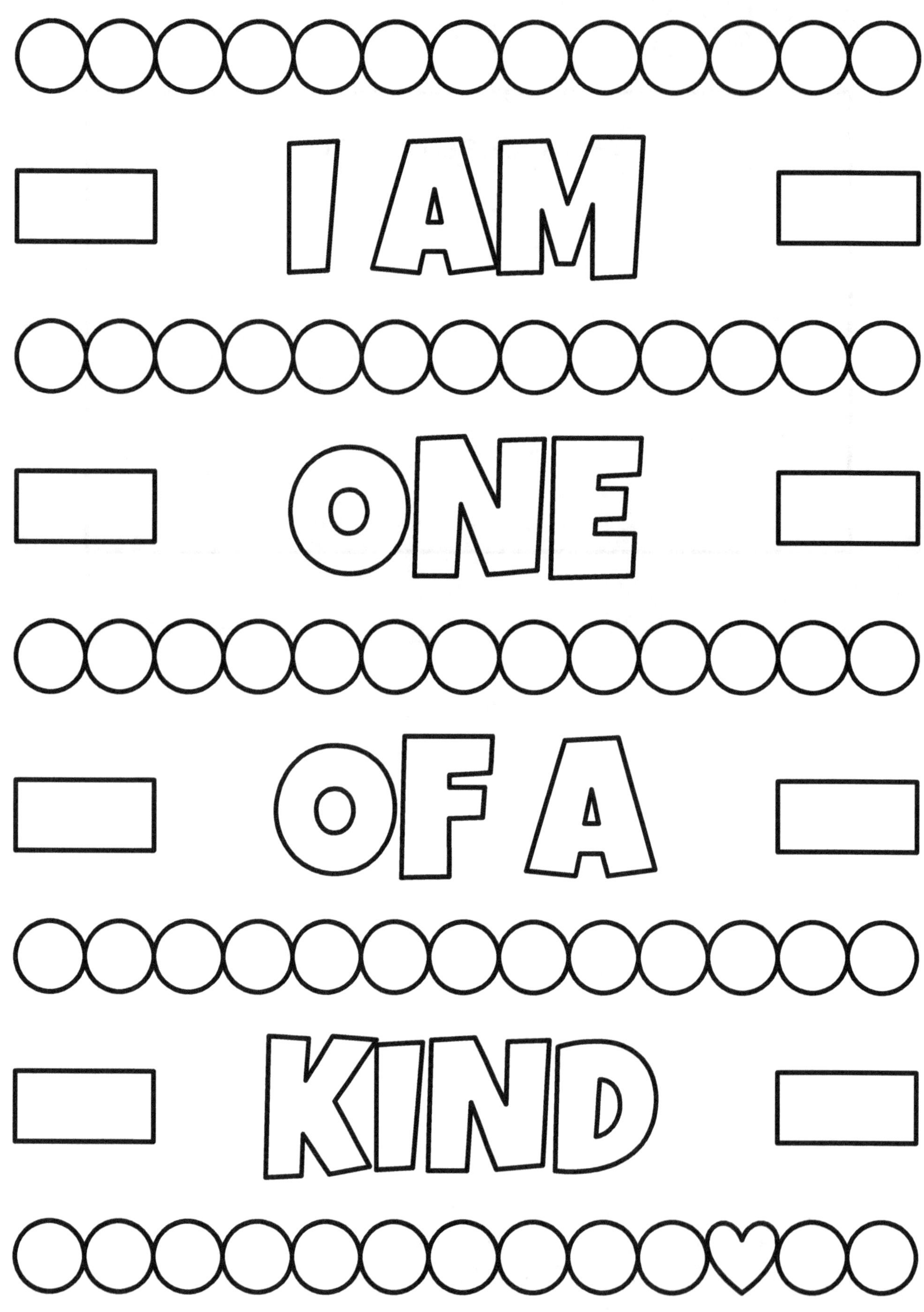

I AM
ONE
OF A
KIND

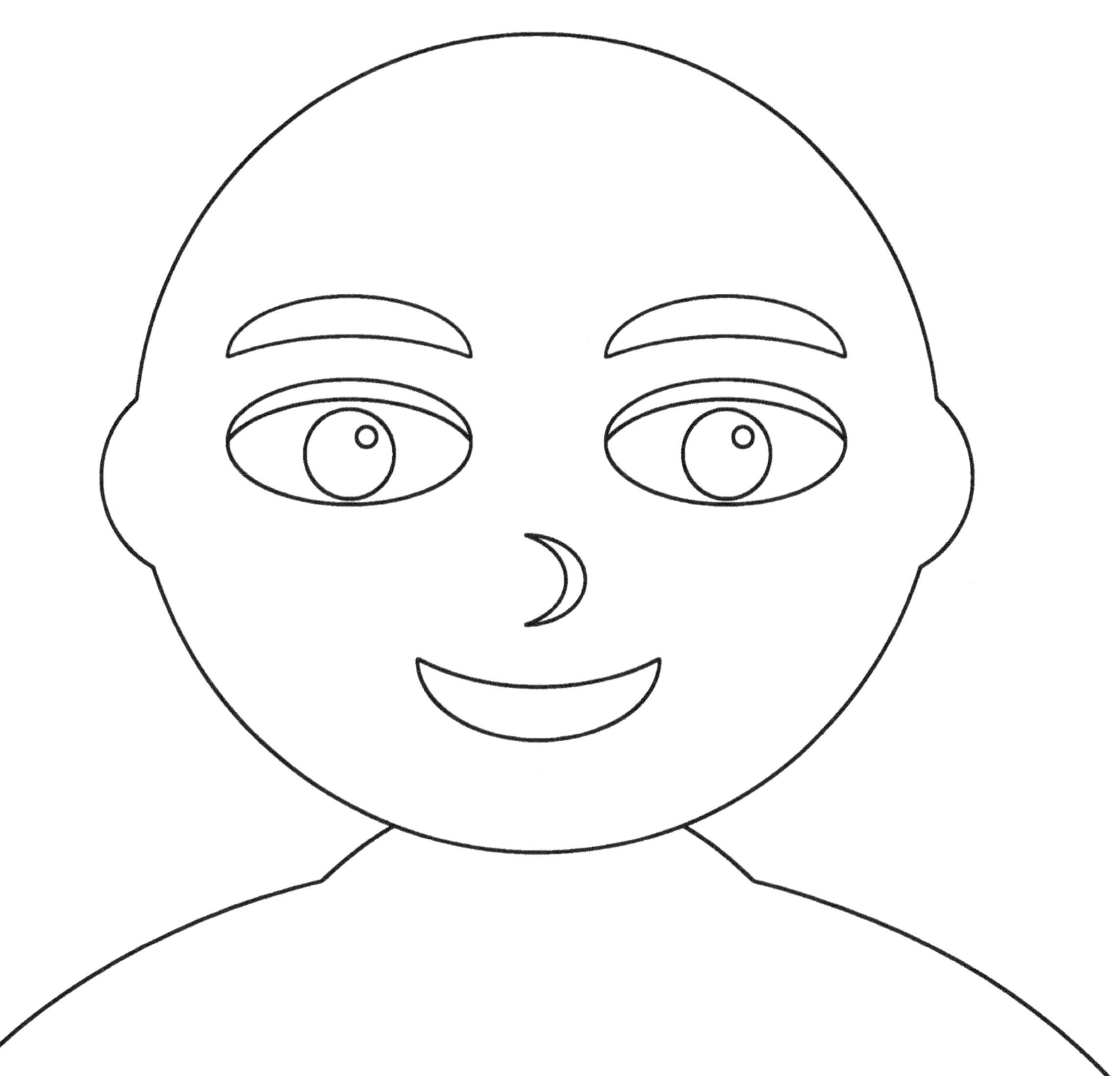

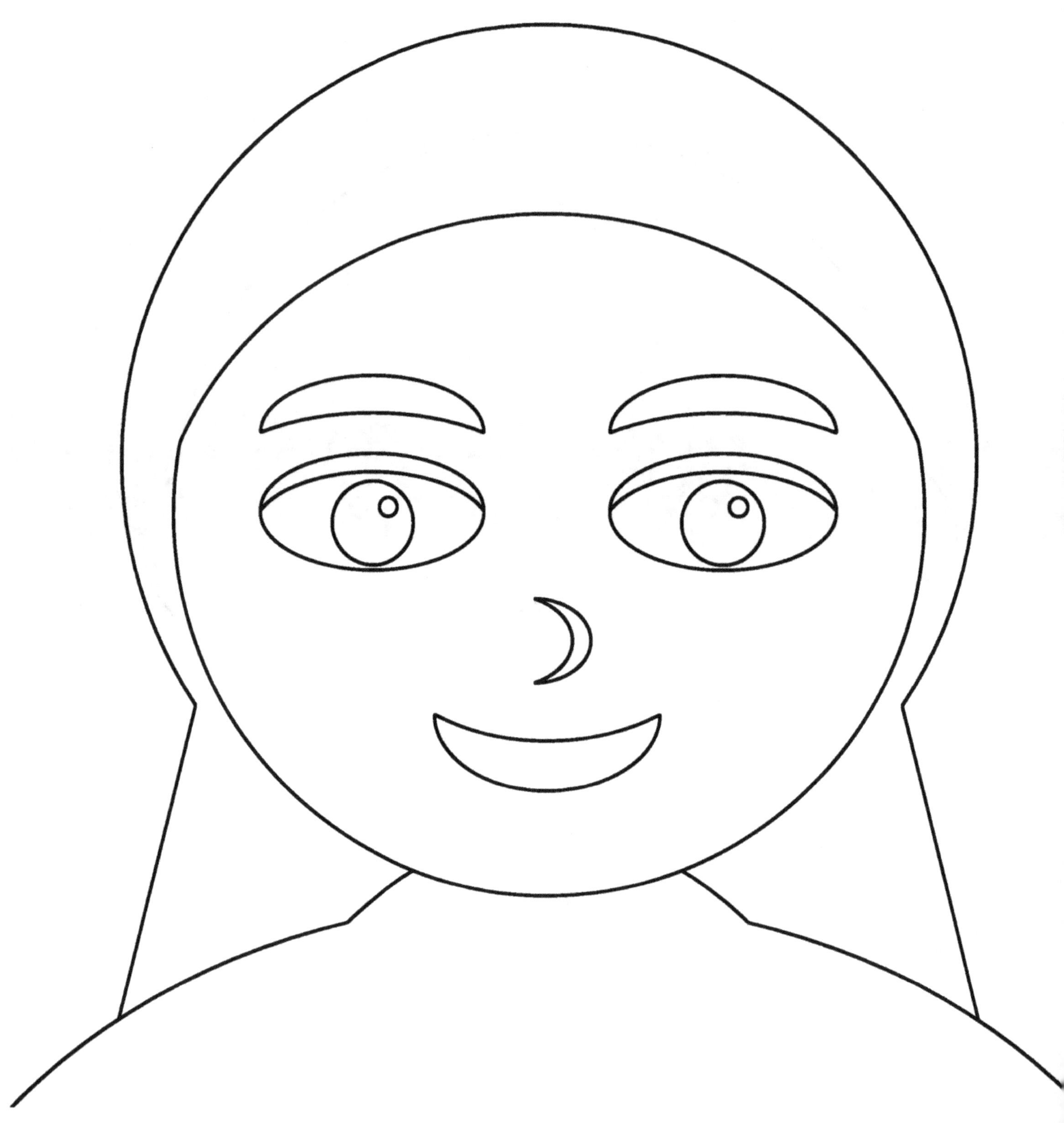

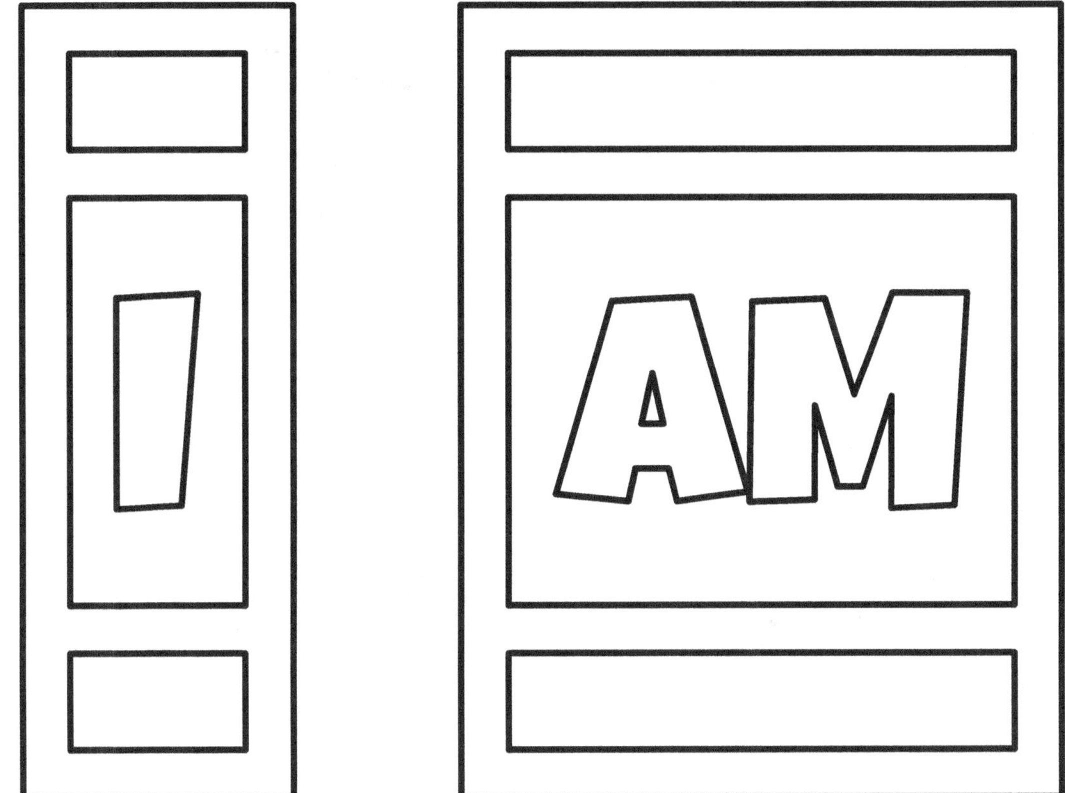
I
AM
STRONG

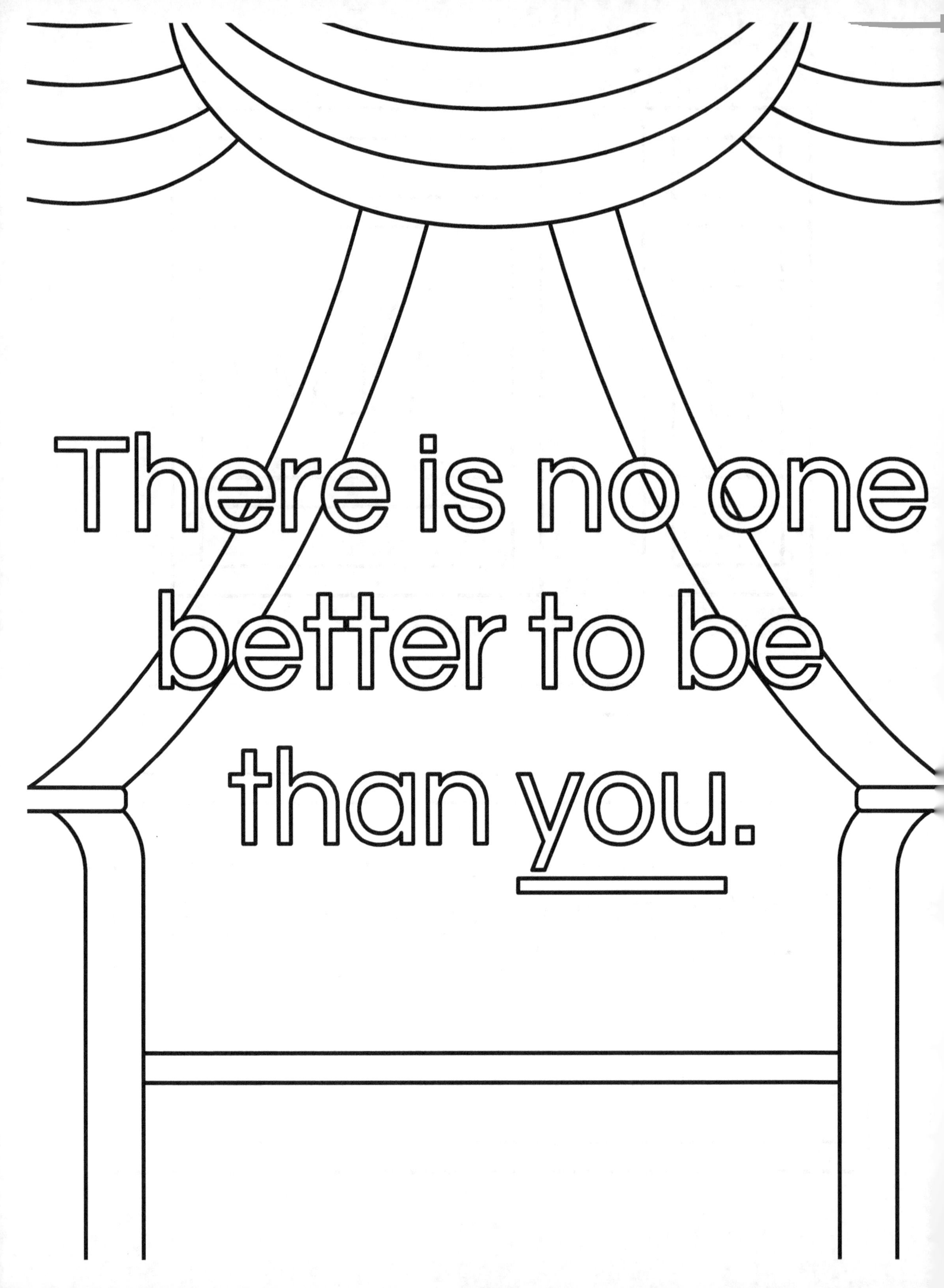

There is no one better to be than you.

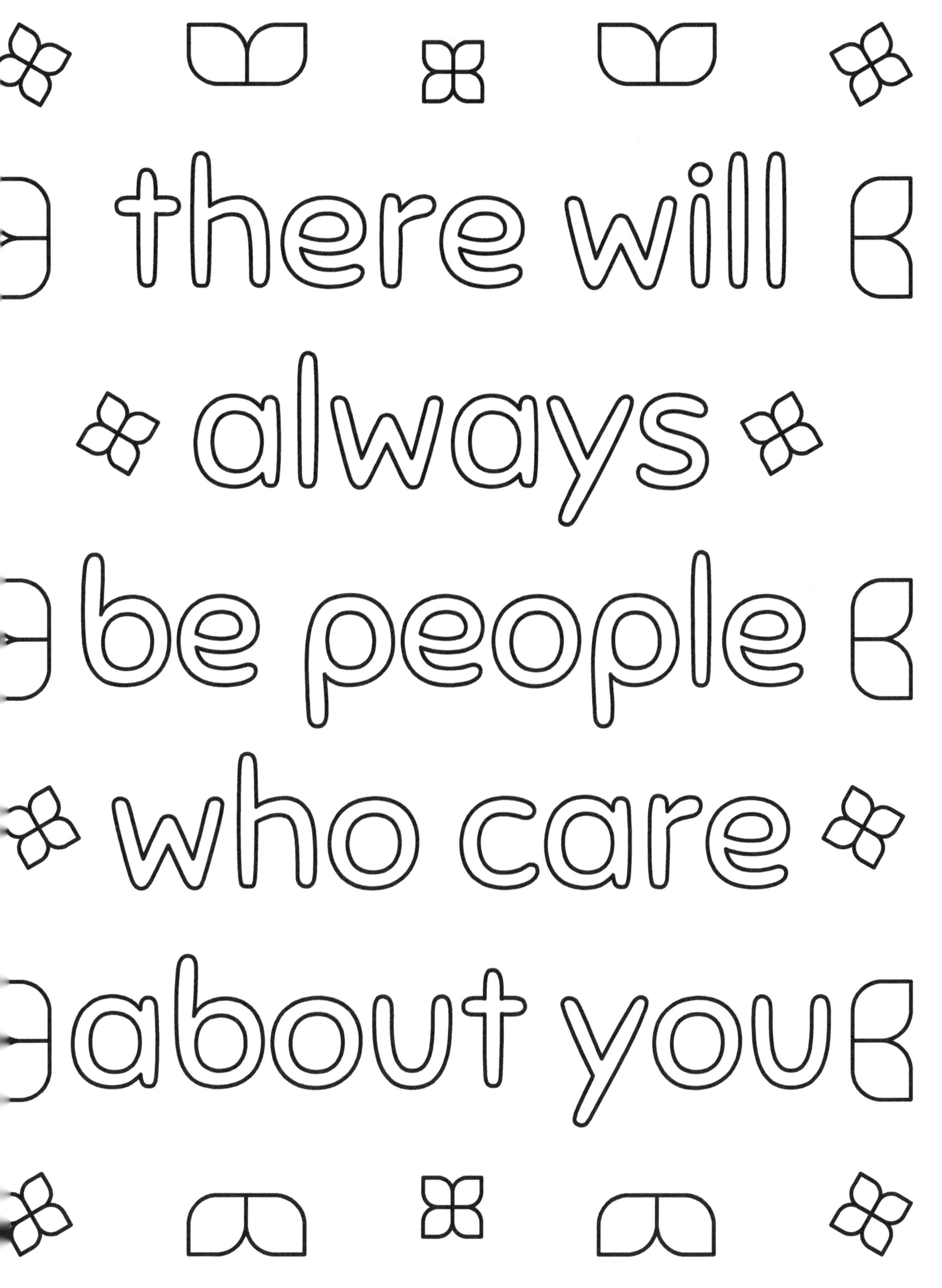

there will
always
be people
who care
about you

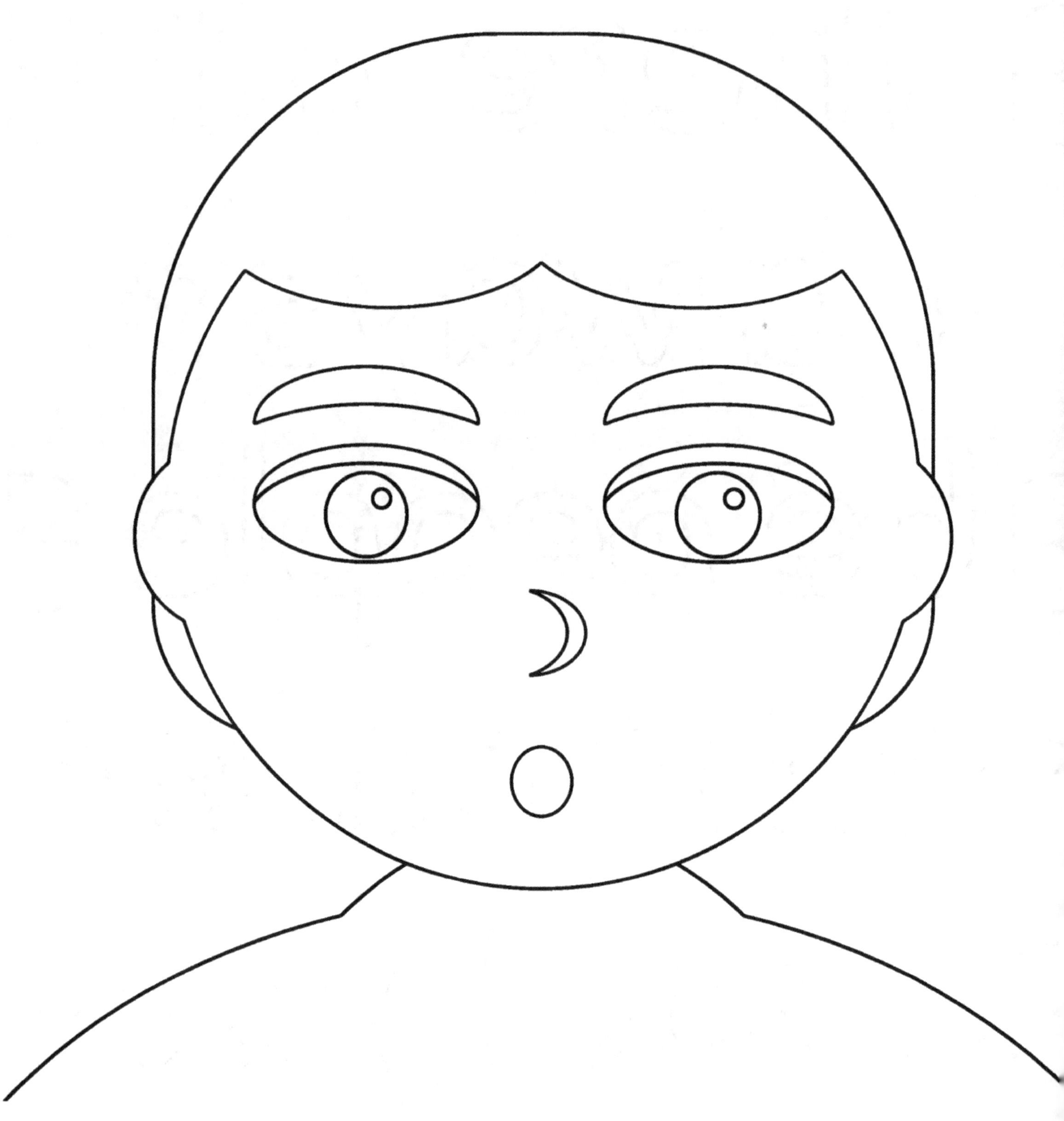

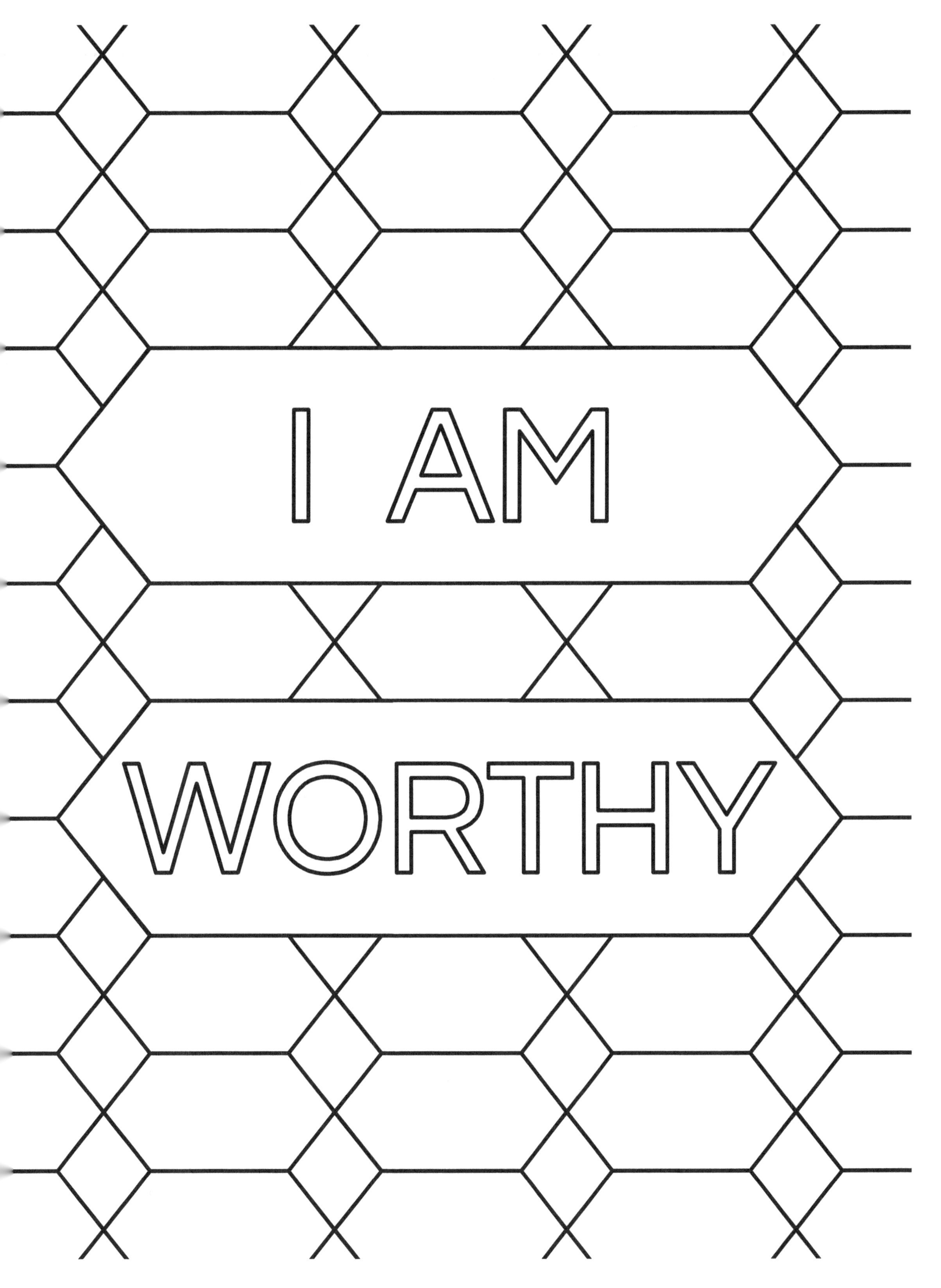

I AM
WORTHY

I AM
BRAVE

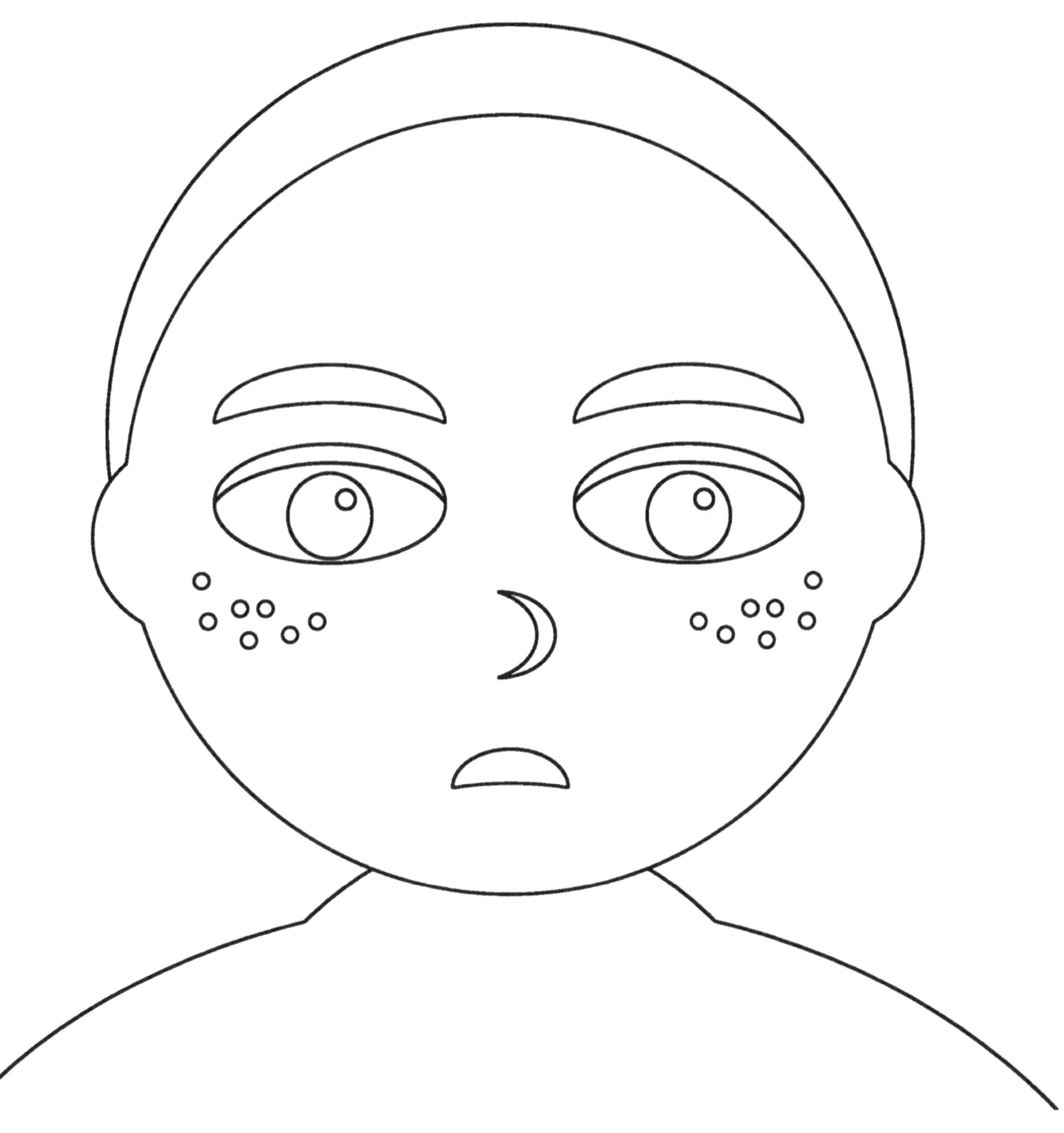

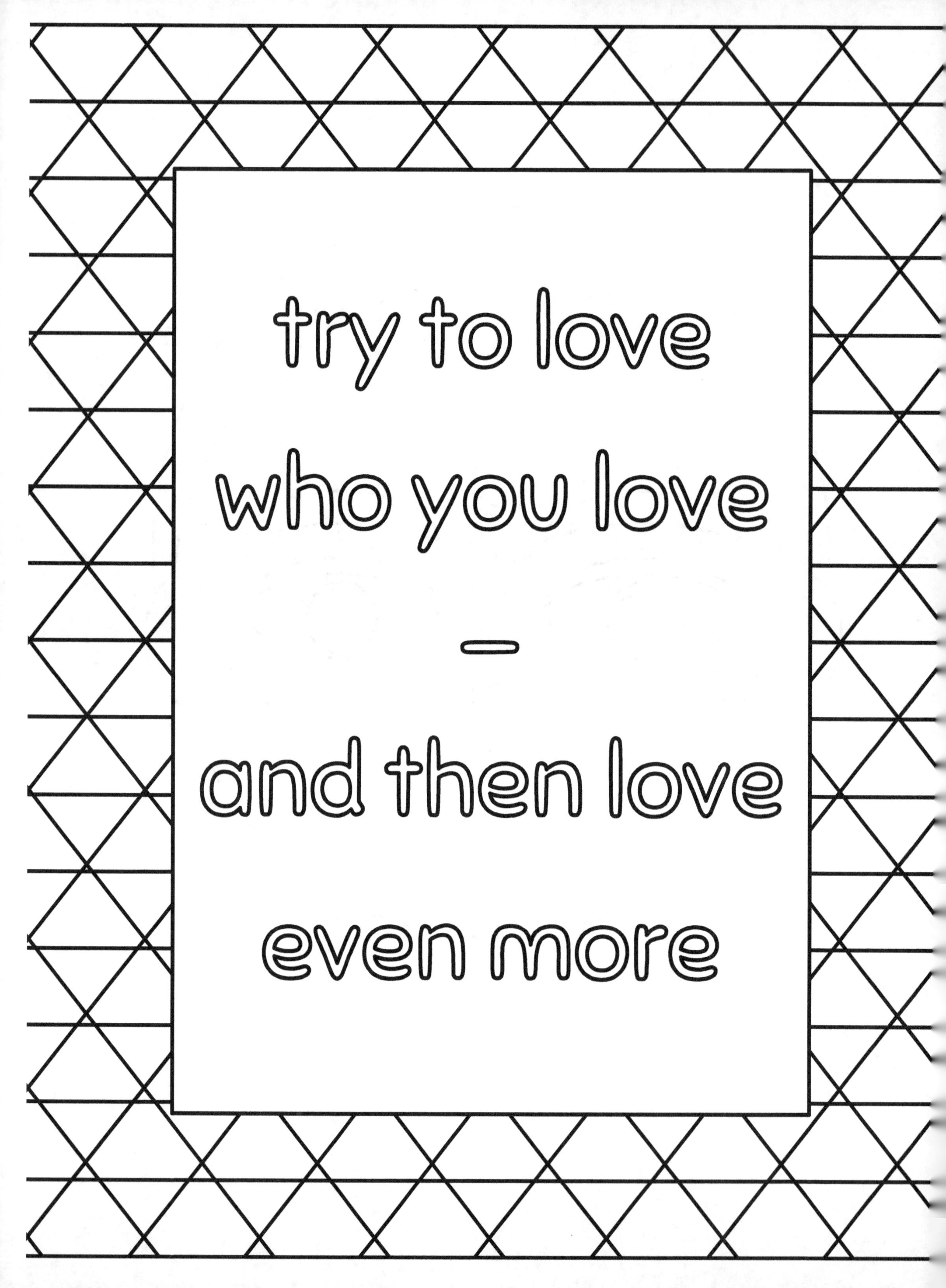

try to love
who you love
–
and then love
even more

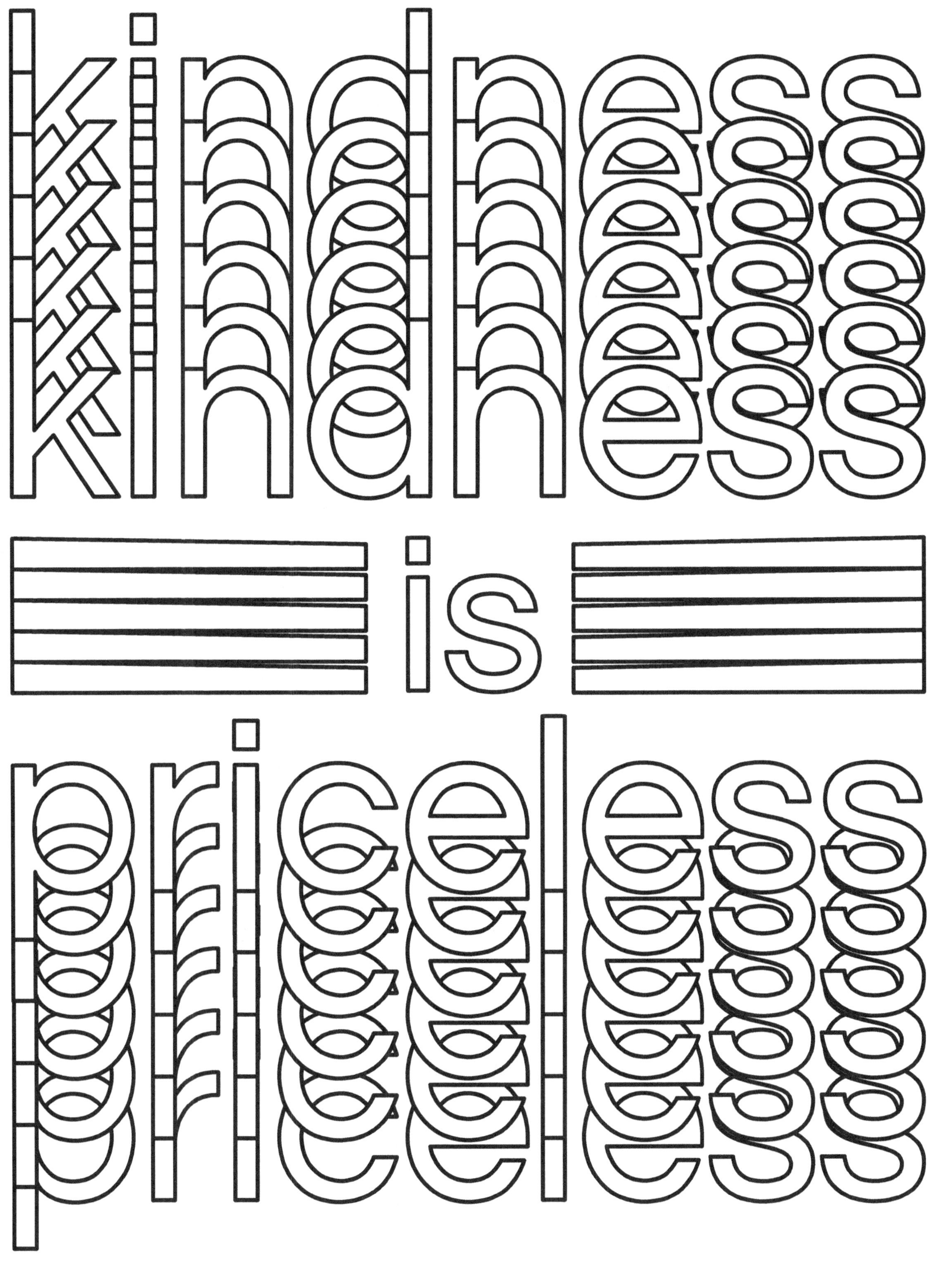

kindness
is
priceless

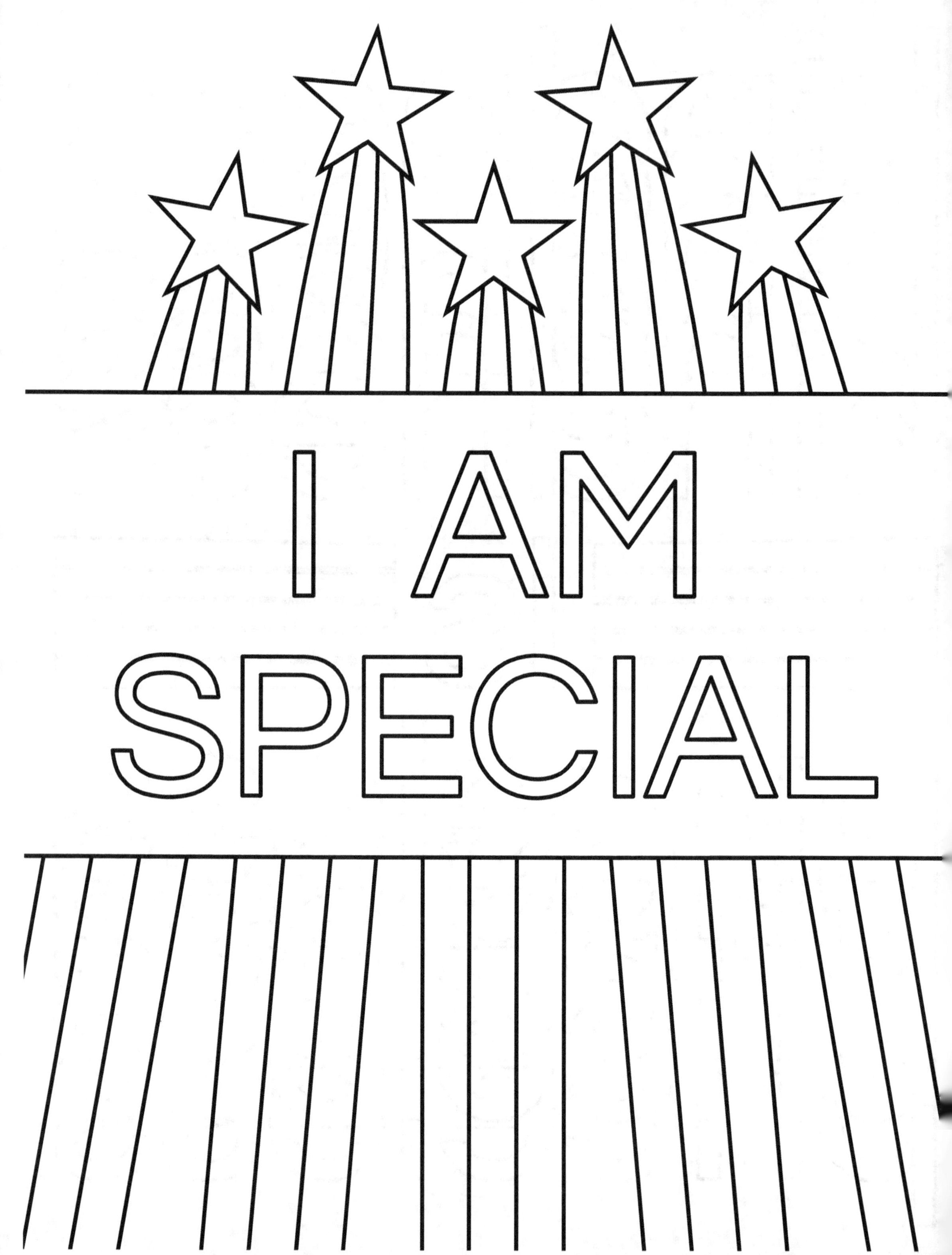

I AM
SPECIAL

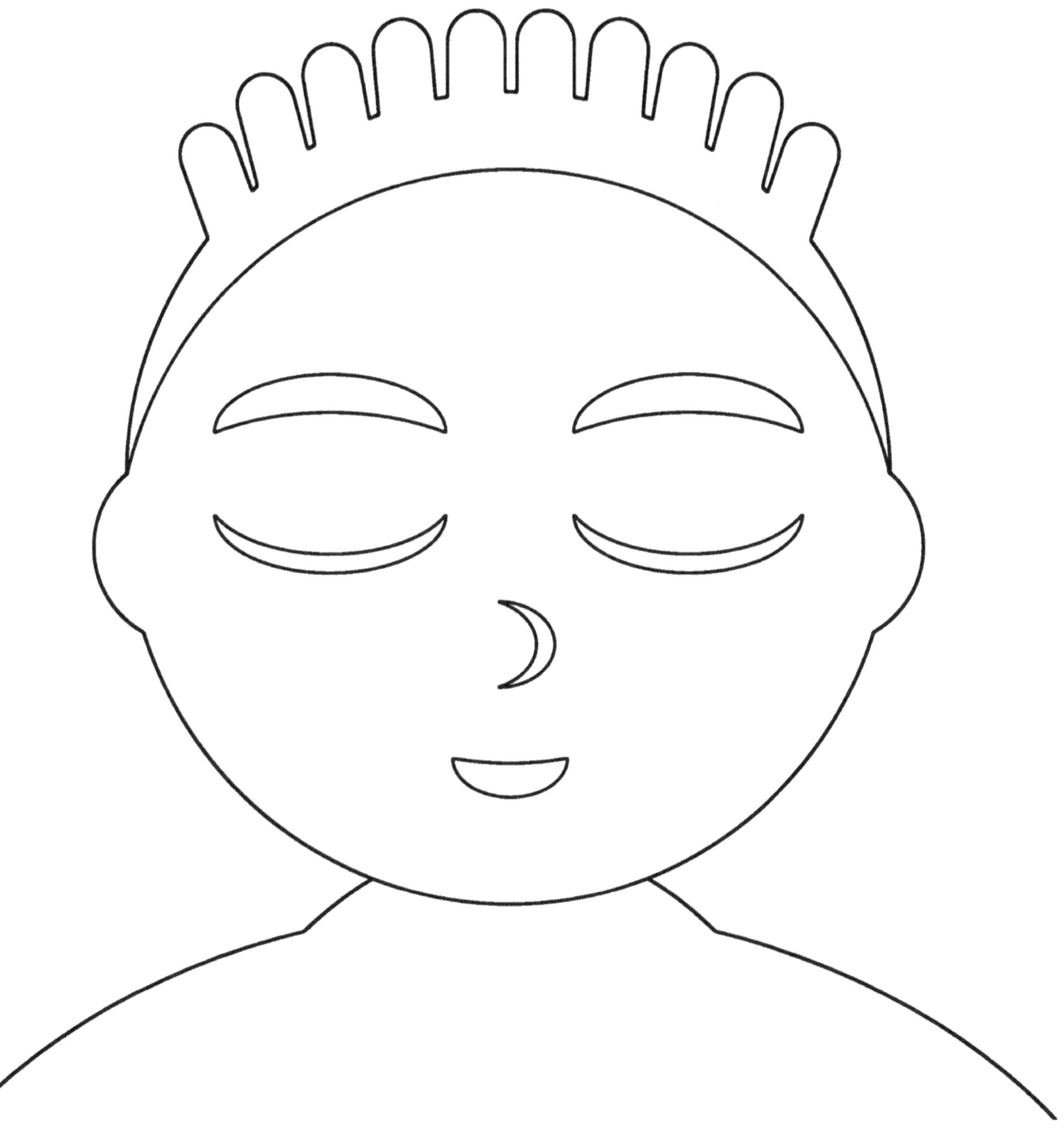

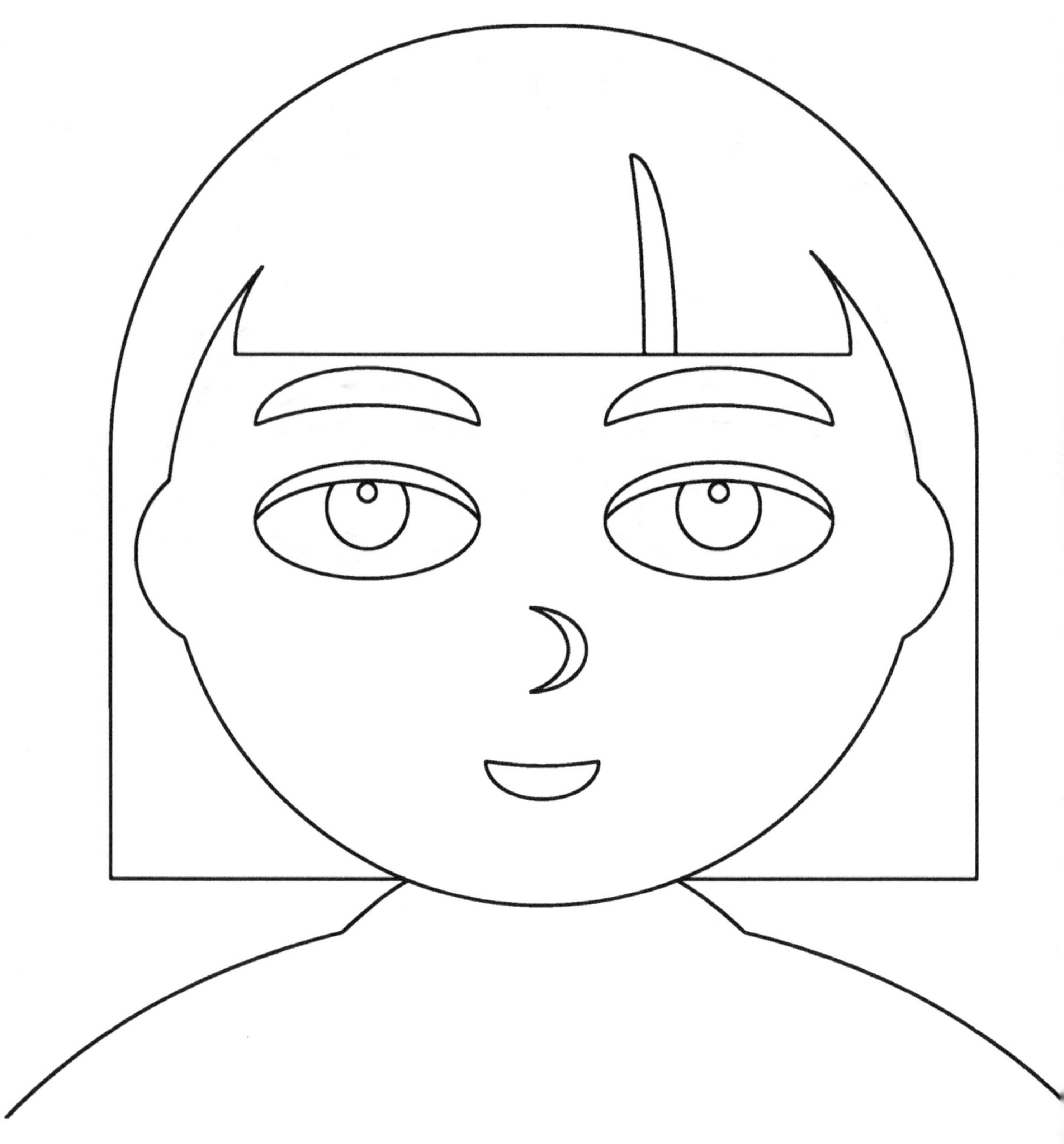

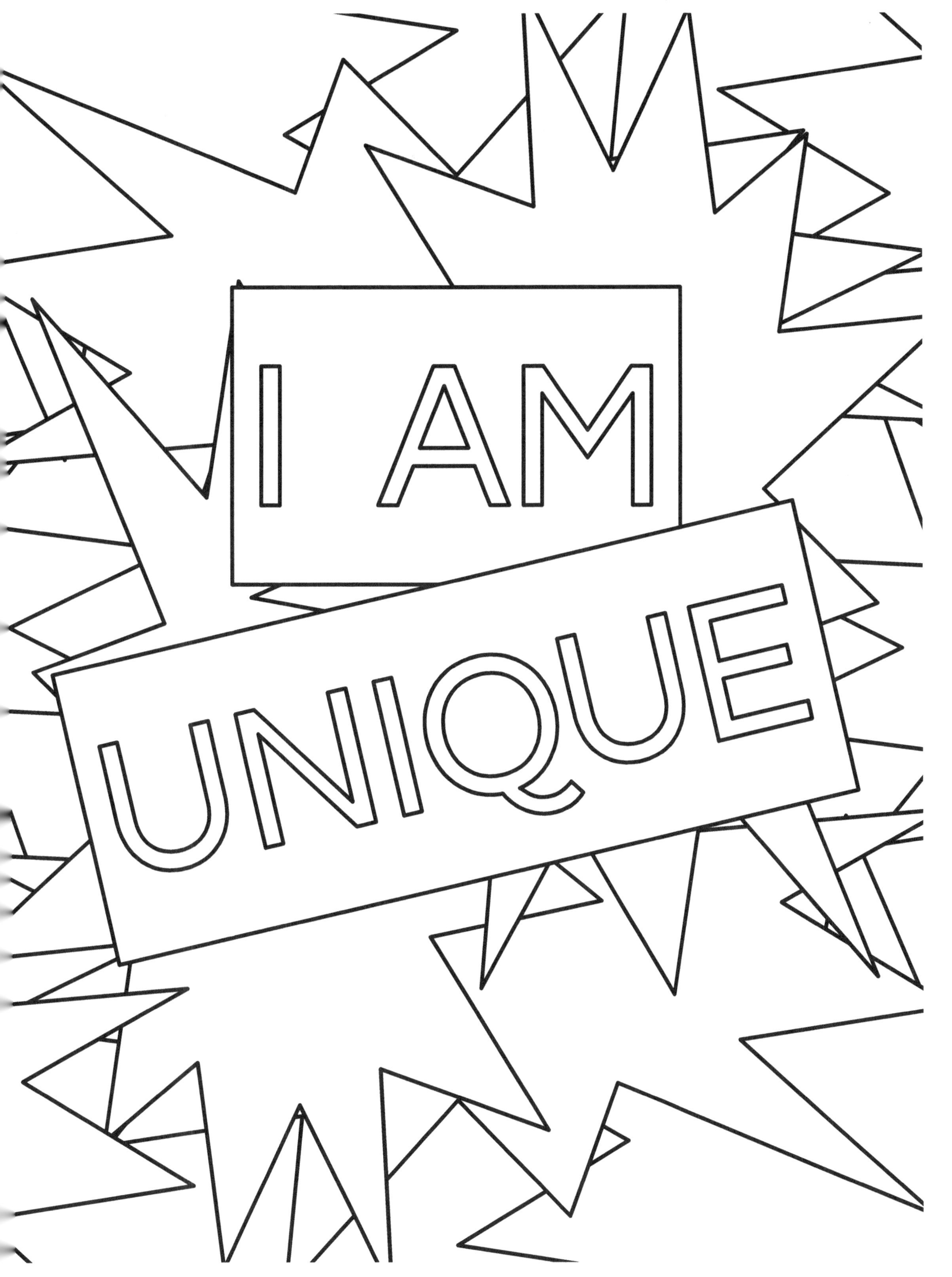

I AM
UNIQUE

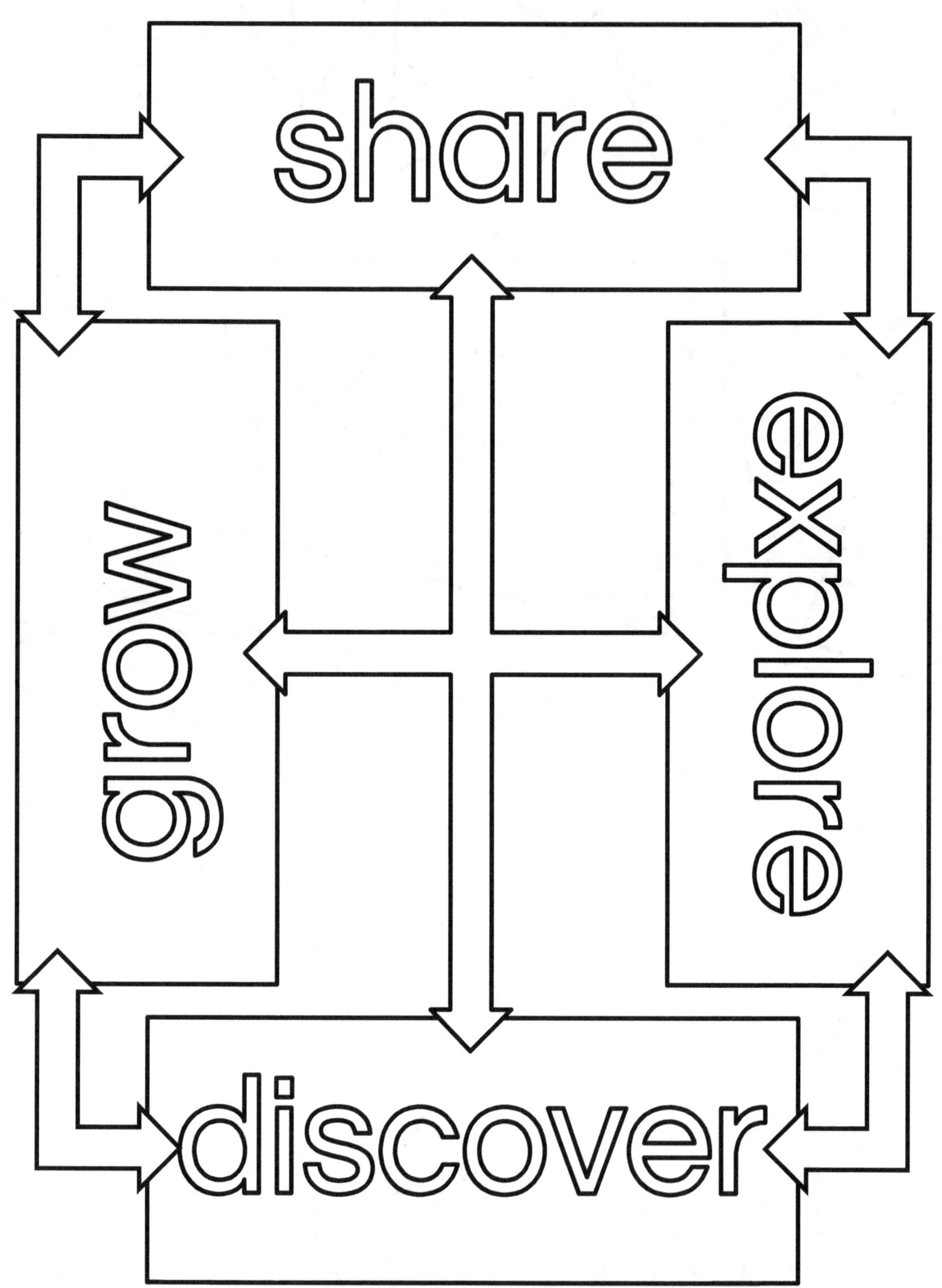

share
grow
explore
discover

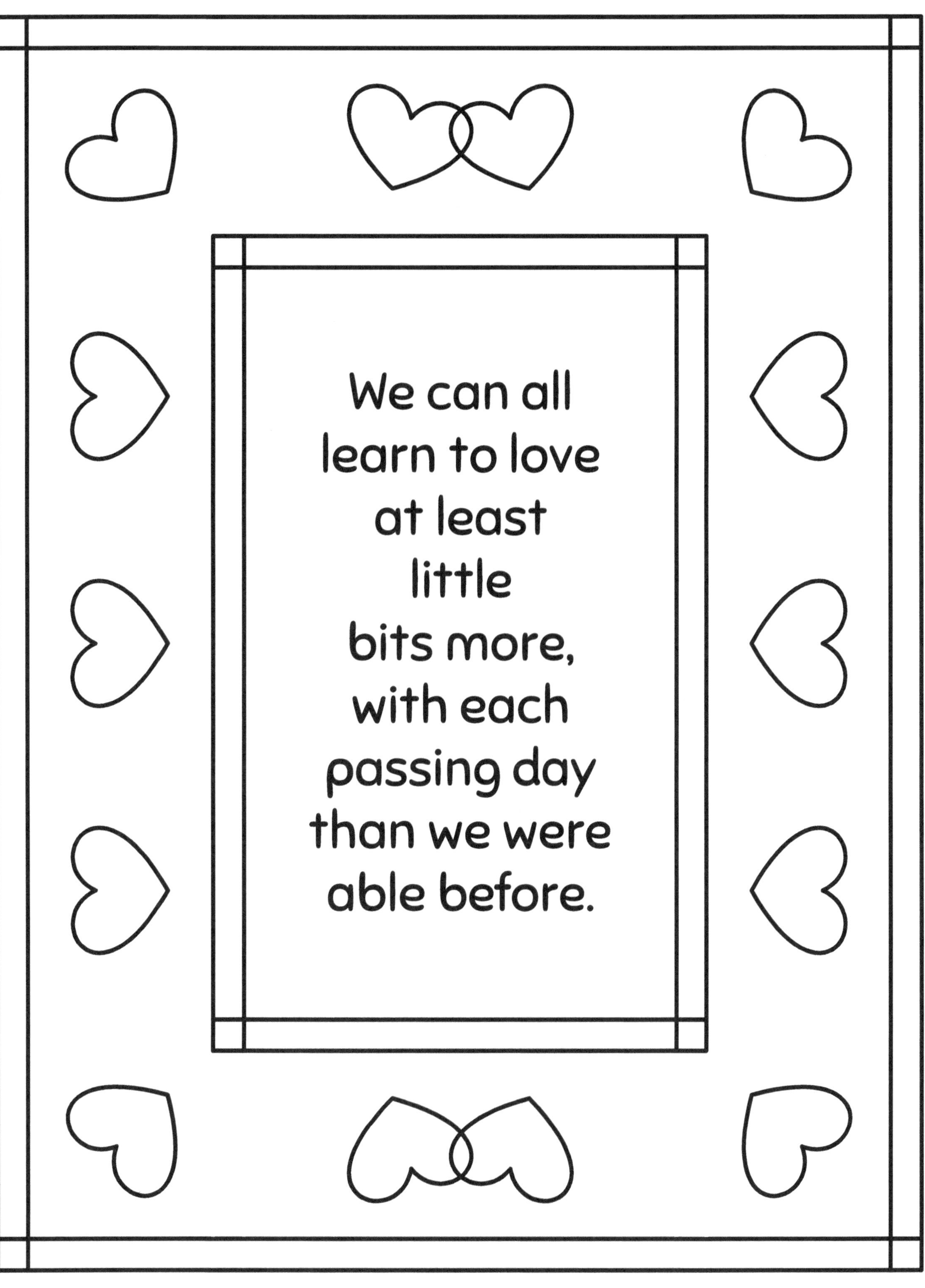

We can all
learn to love
at least
little
bits more,
with each
passing day
than we were
able before.

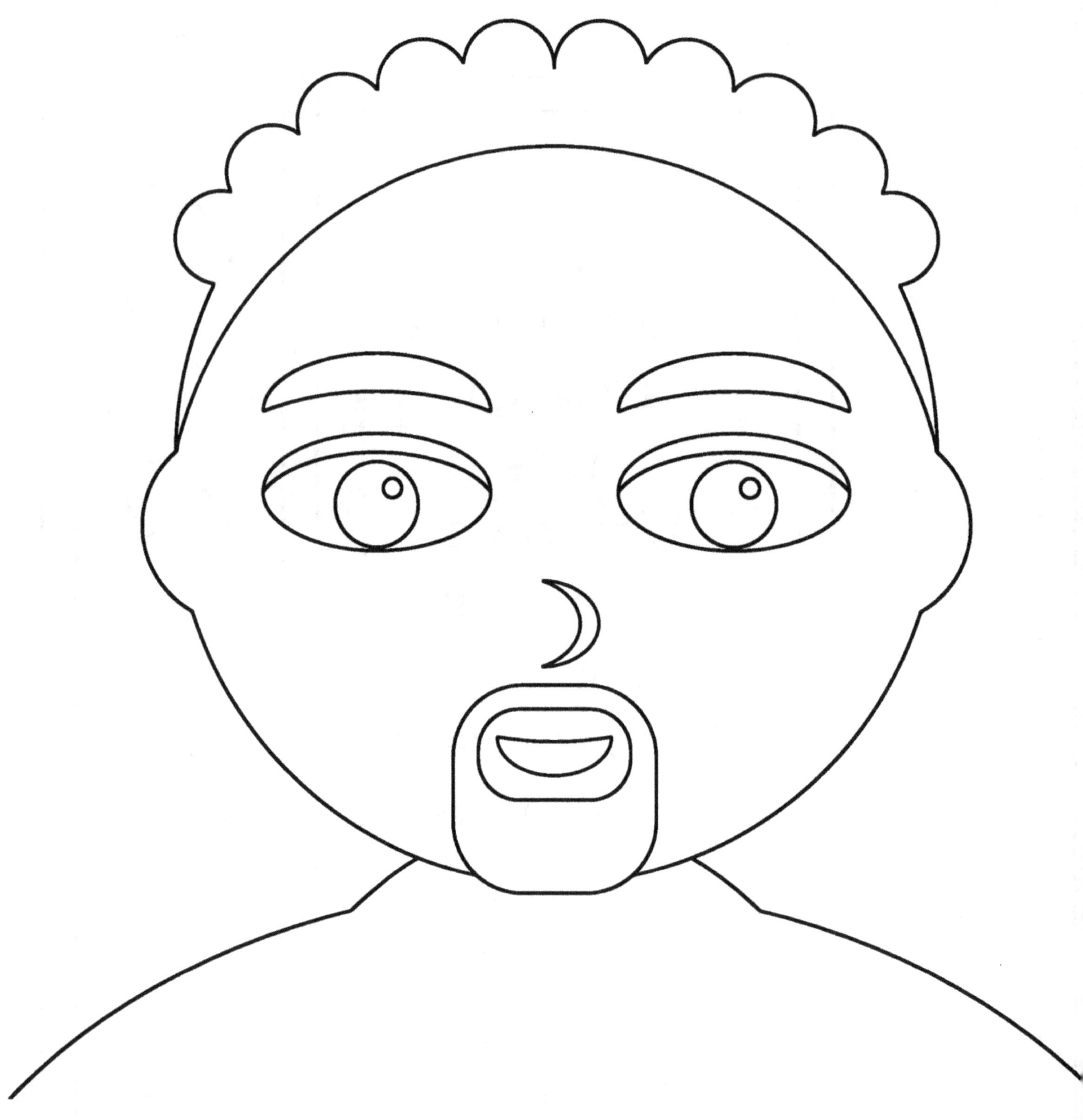

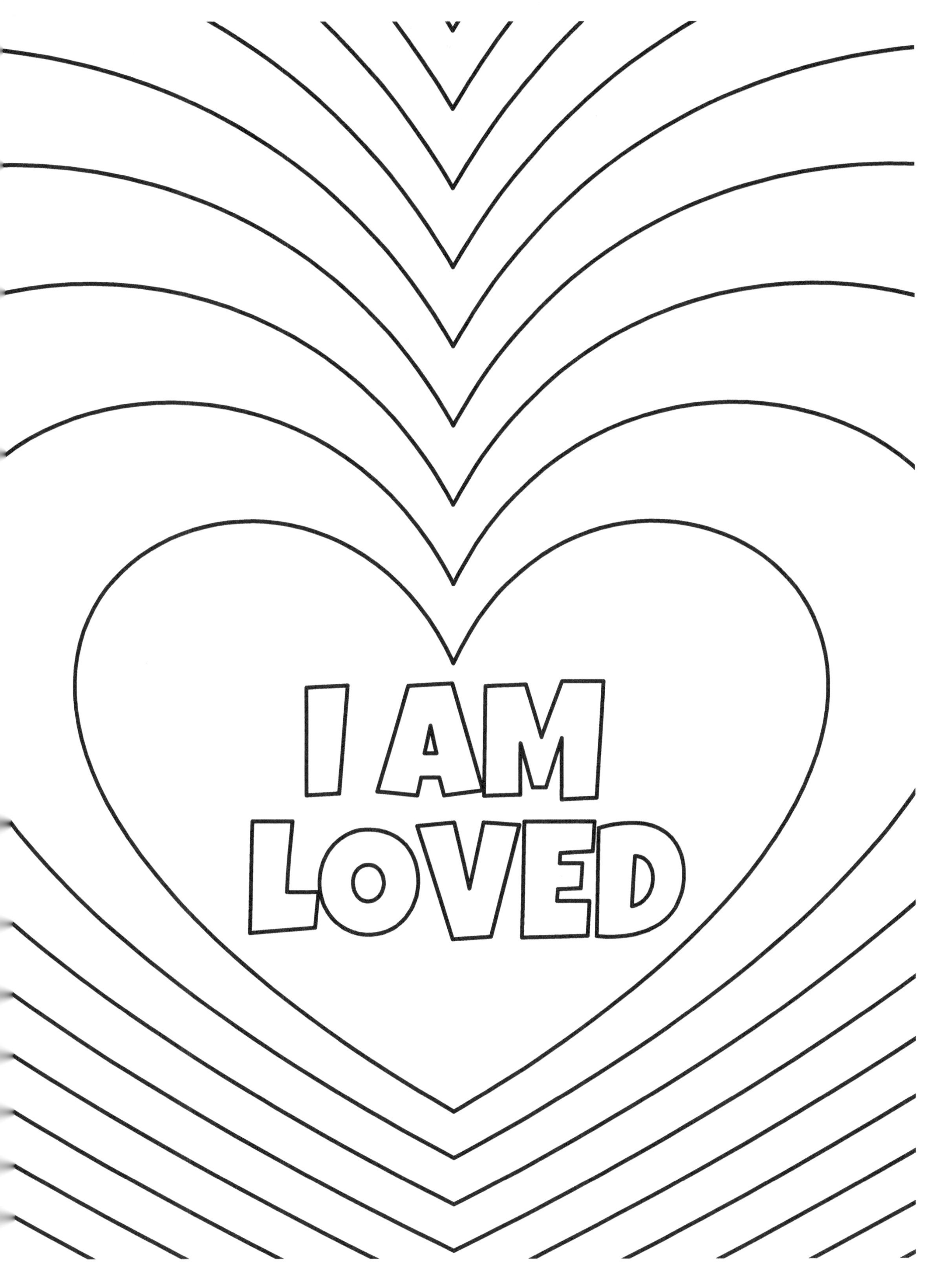

I AM
LOVED

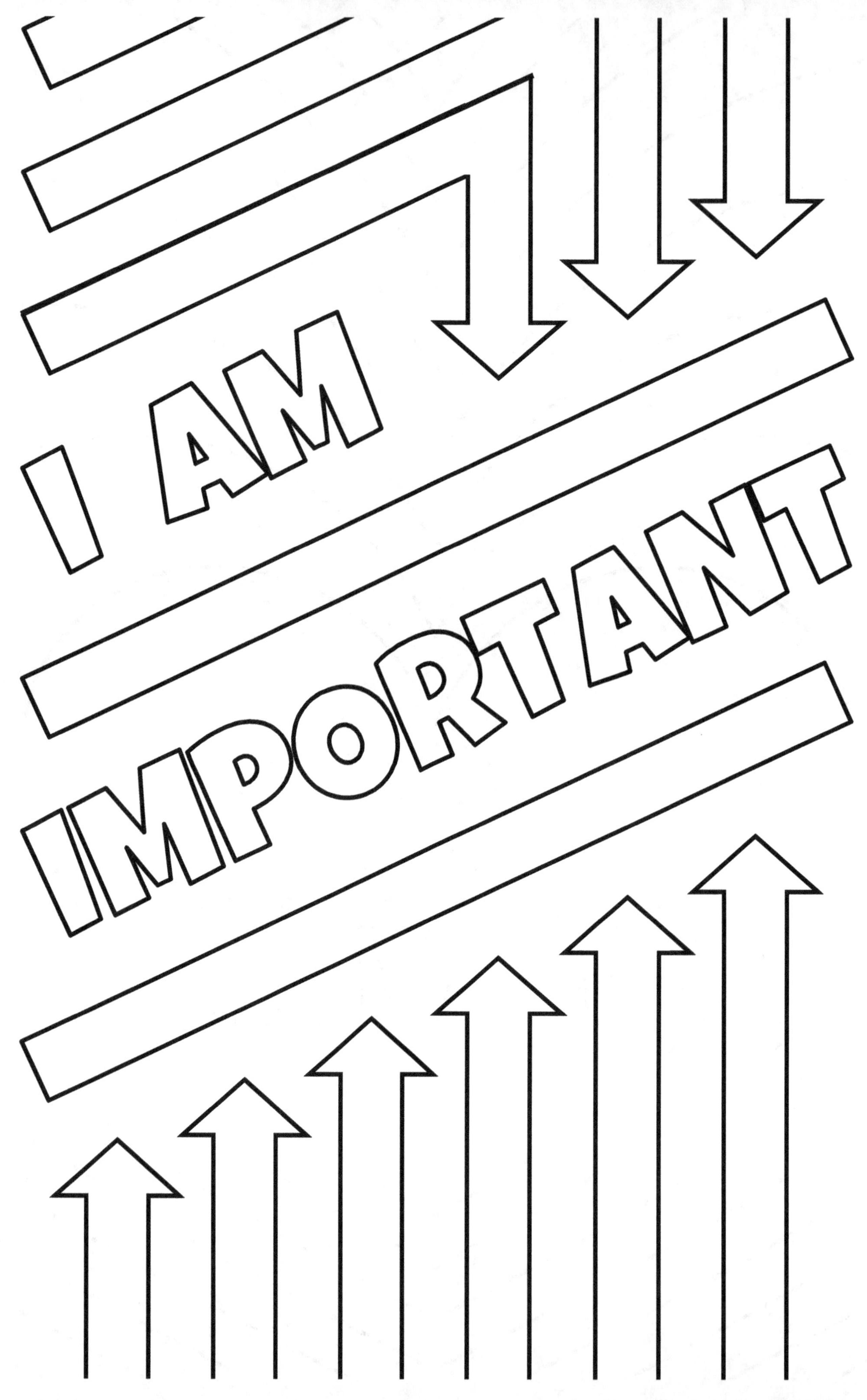

I AM
IMPORTANT

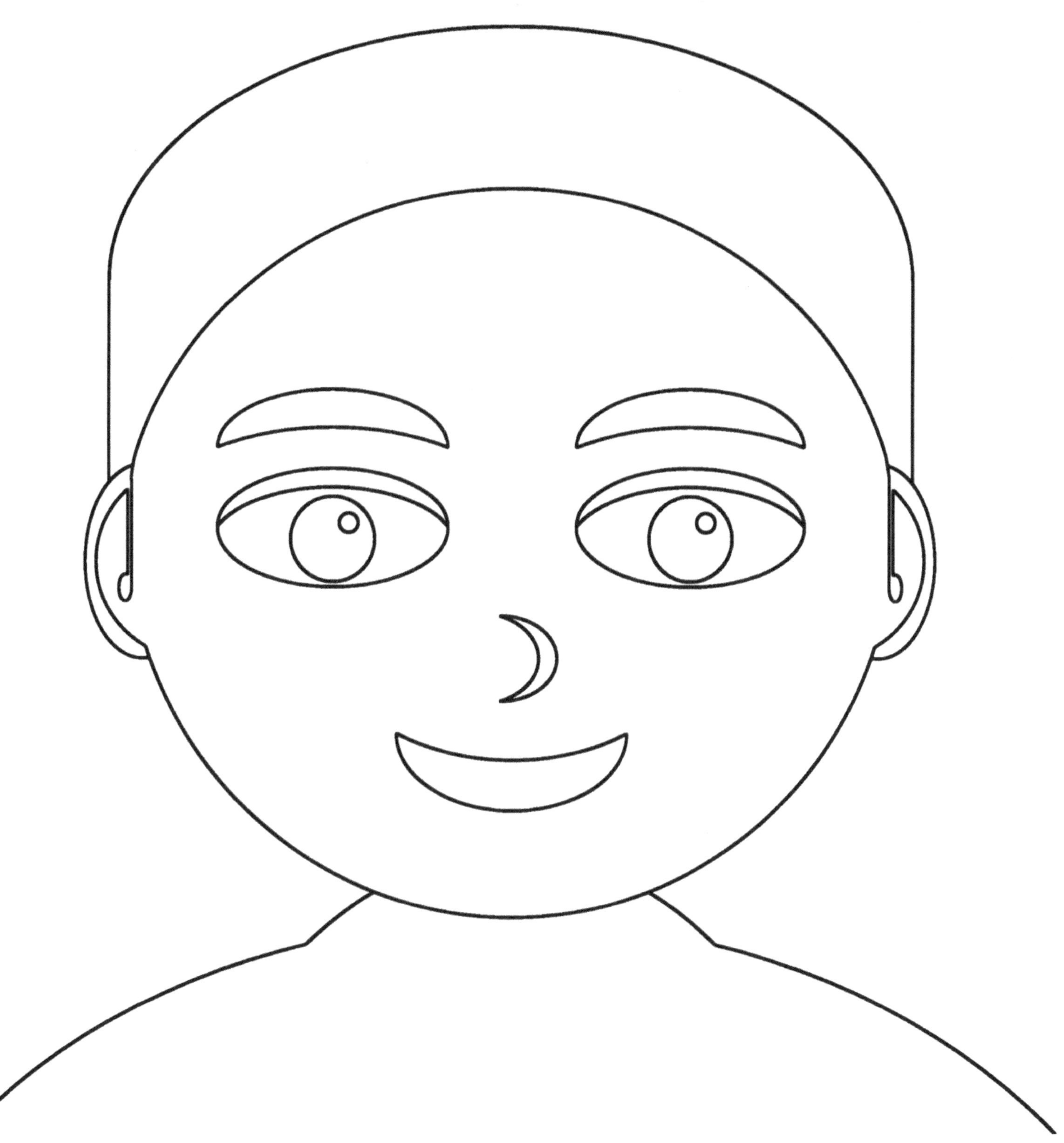

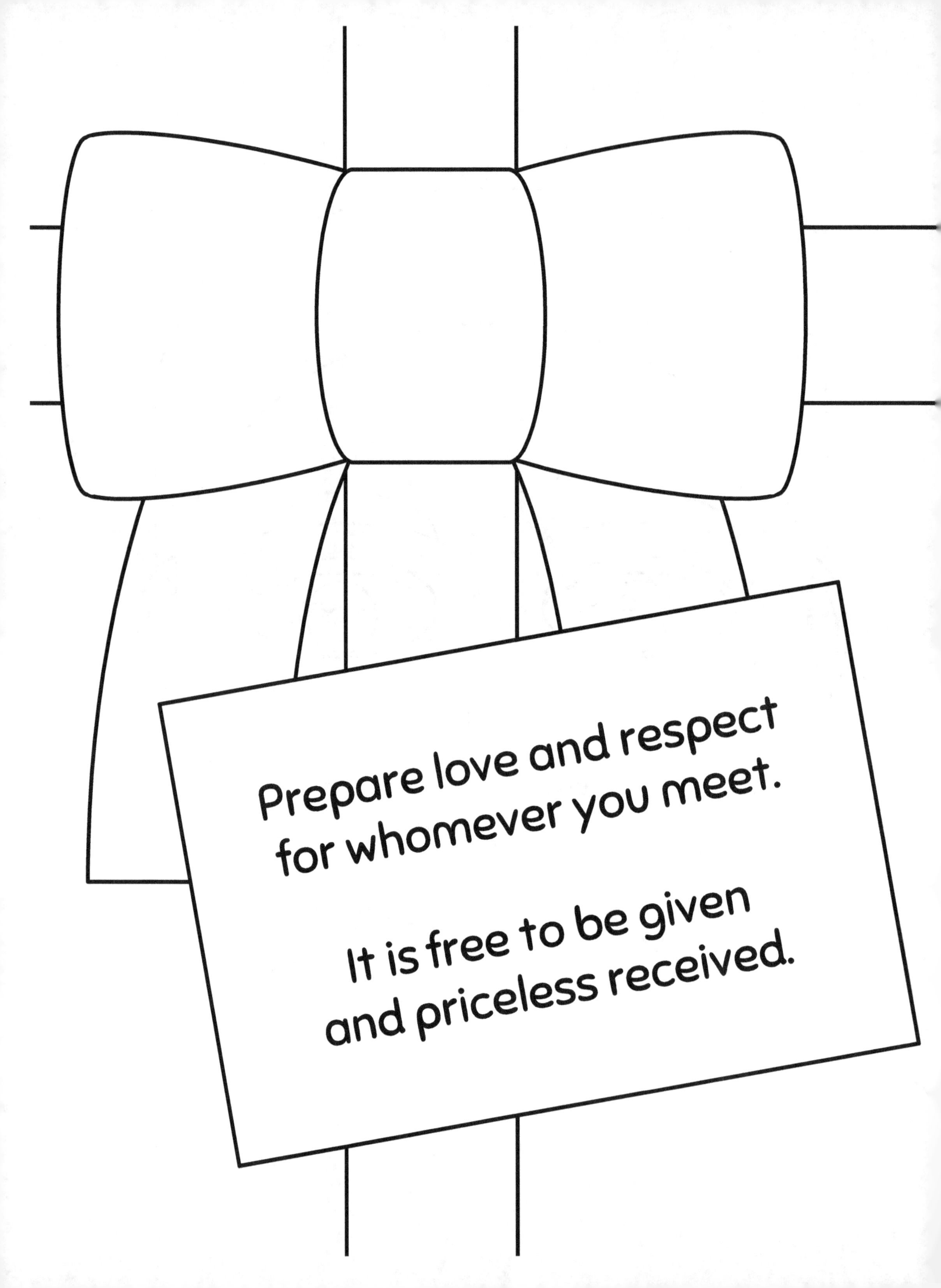
Prepare love and respect
for whomever you meet.

It is free to be given
and priceless received.

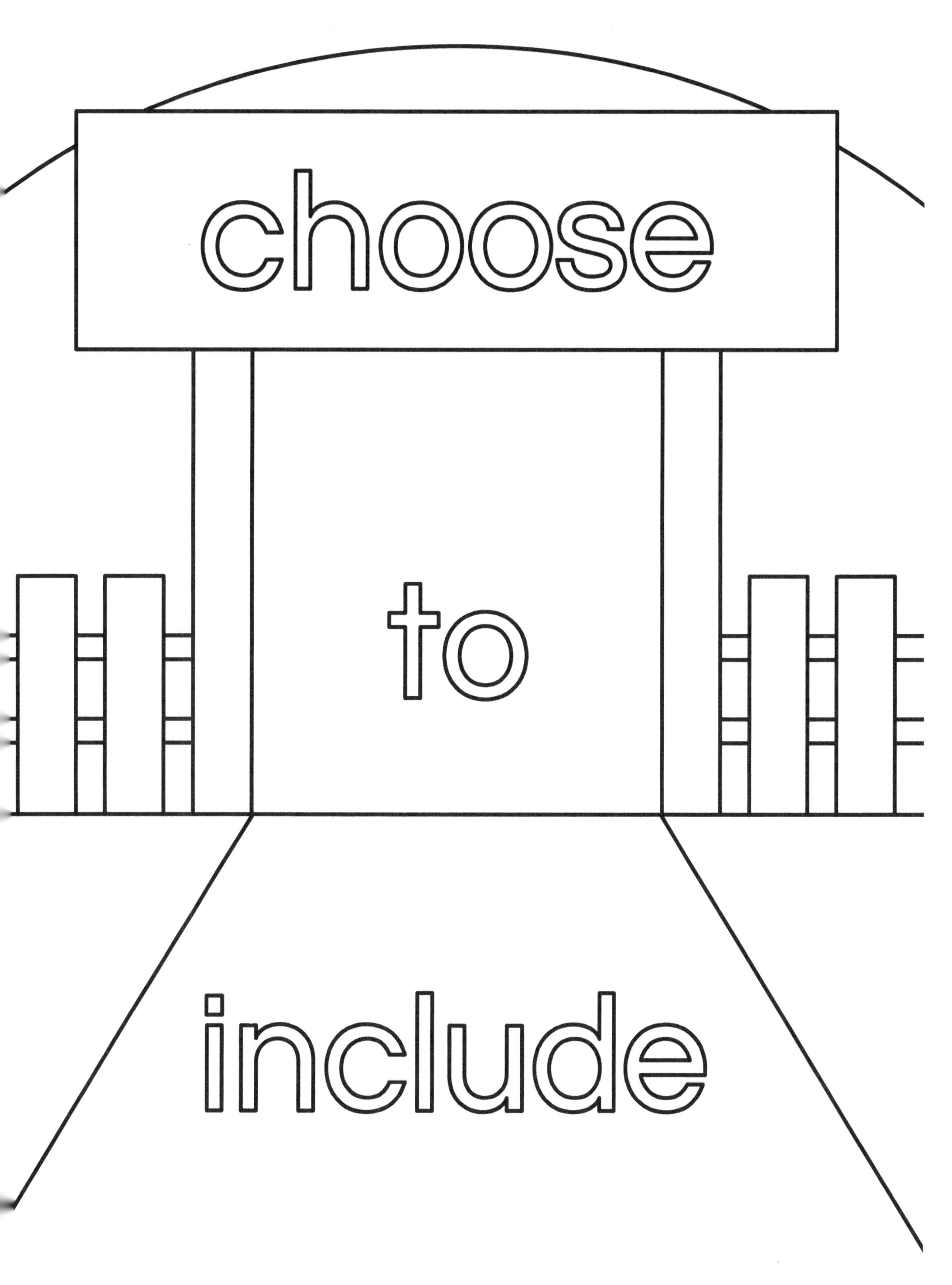

choose
to
include

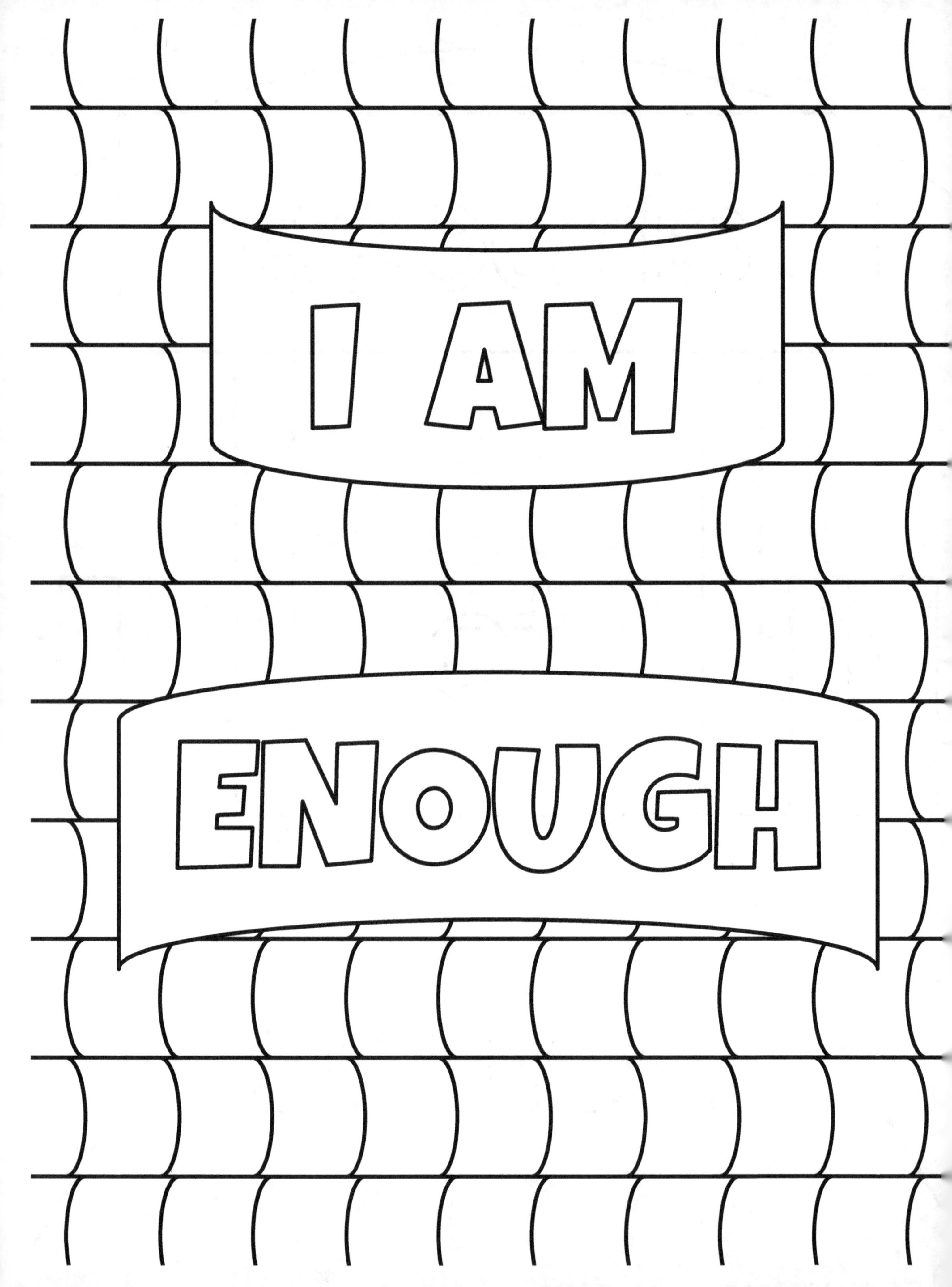

I AM
ENOUGH

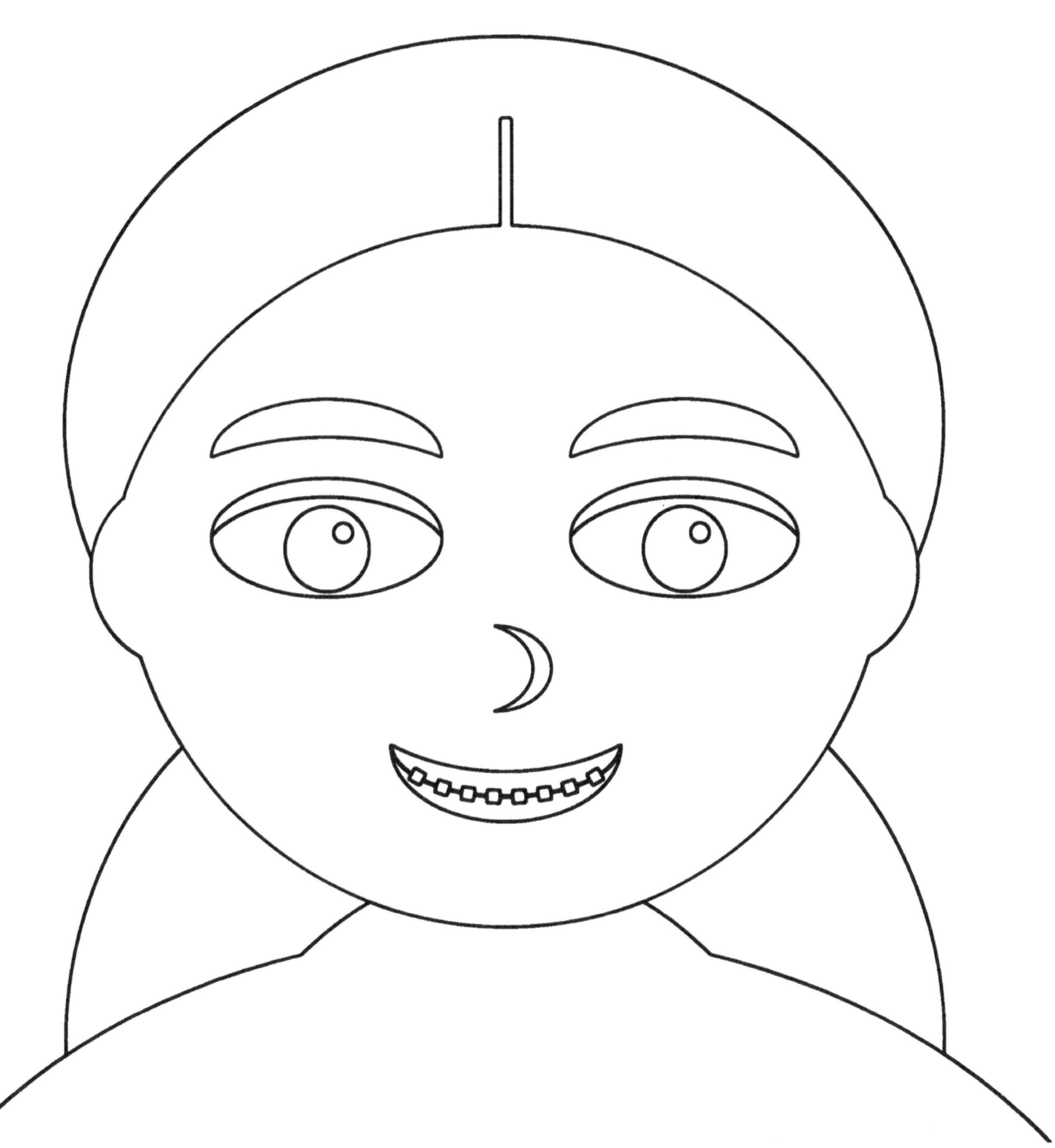

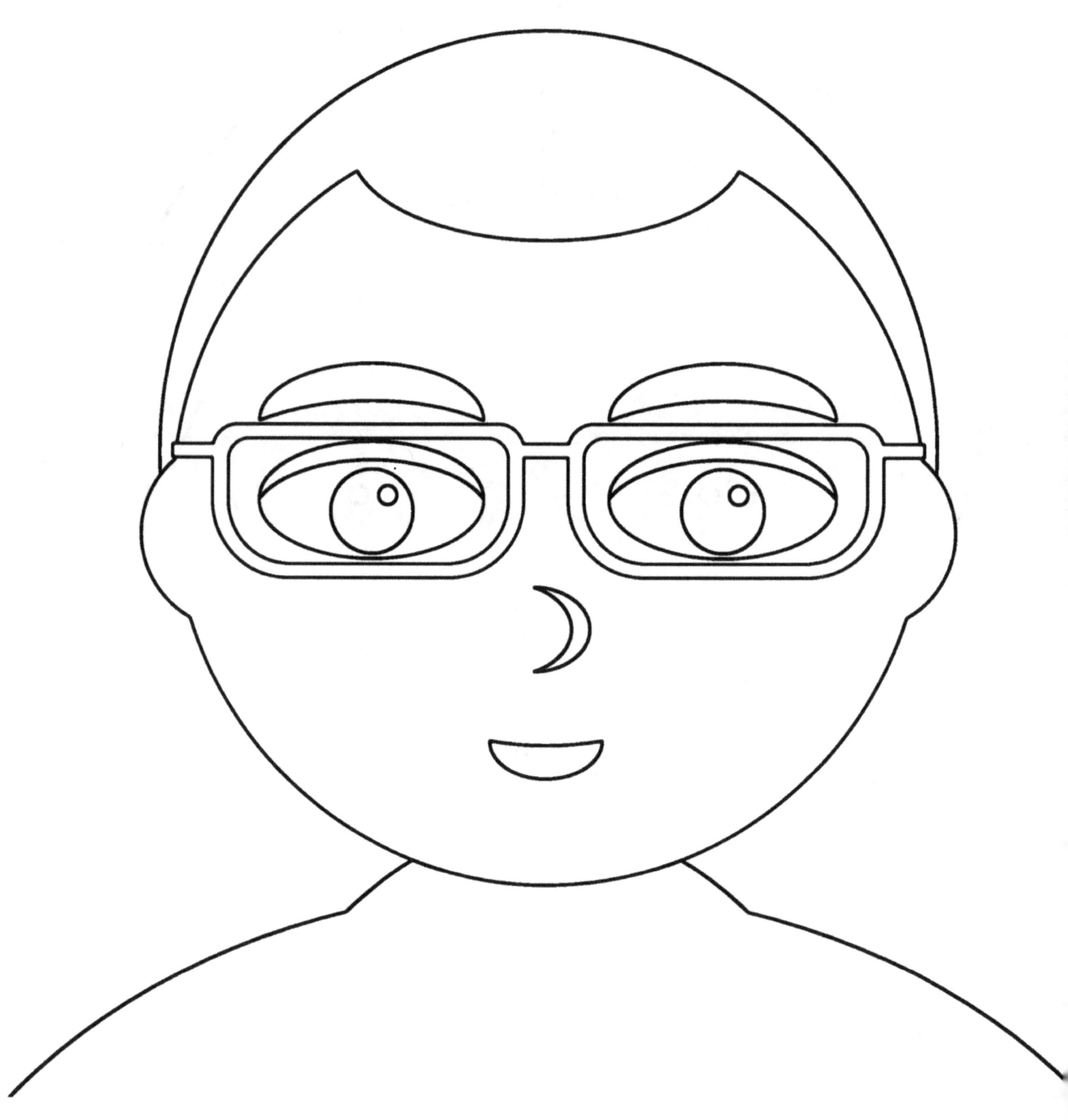

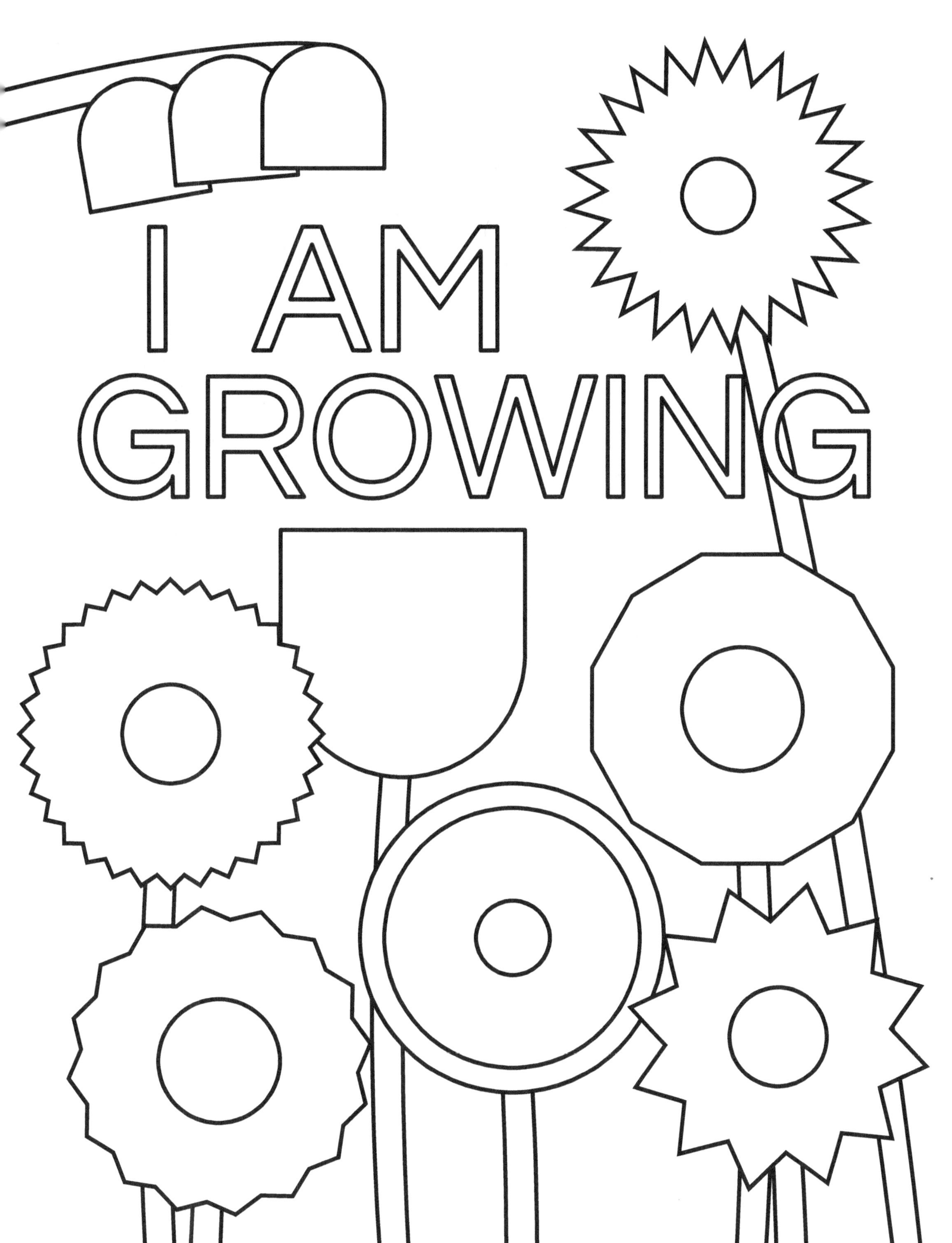

I AM GROWING

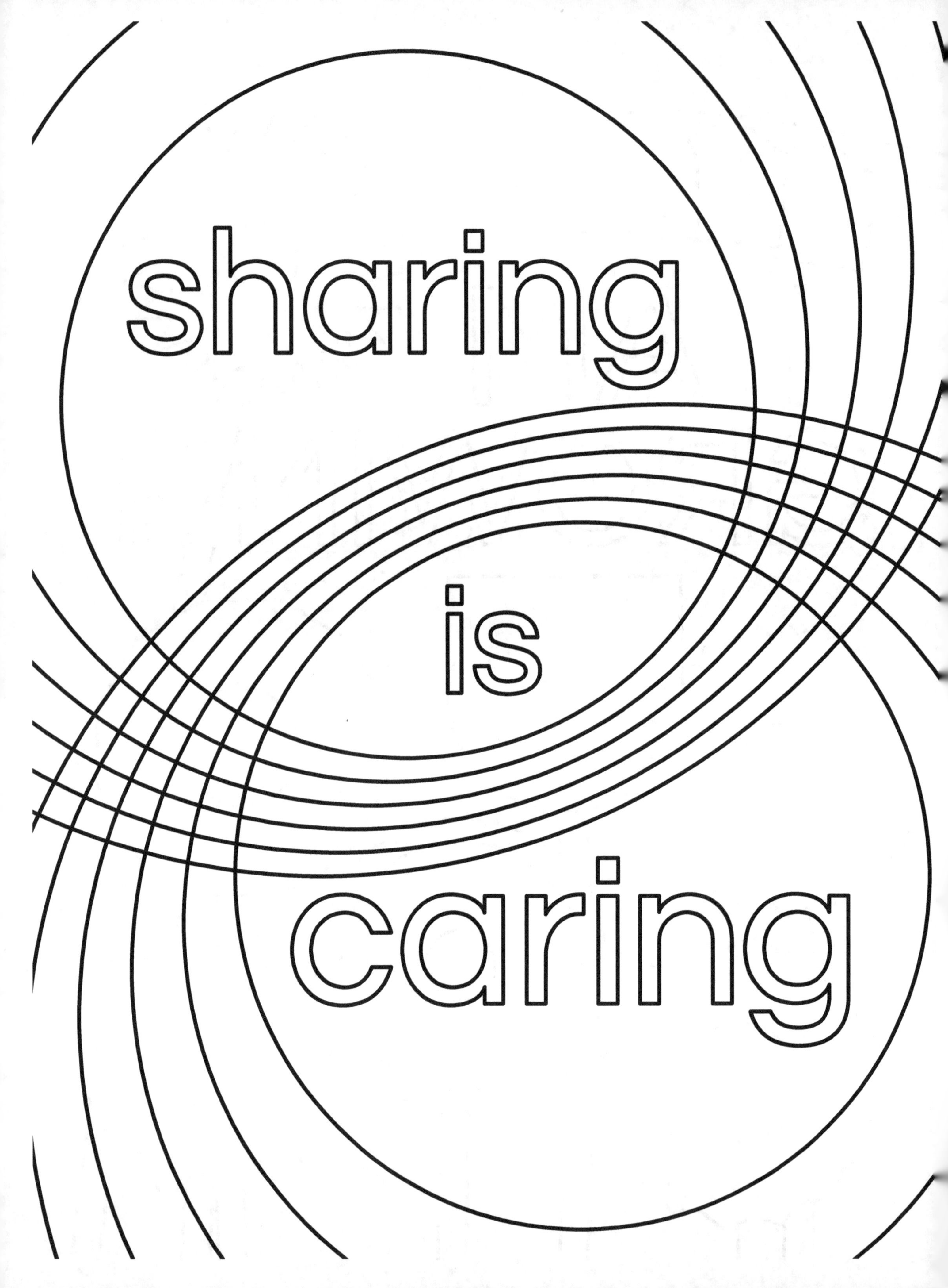
sharing
is
caring

somebody
somewhere
loves you
more than
you know

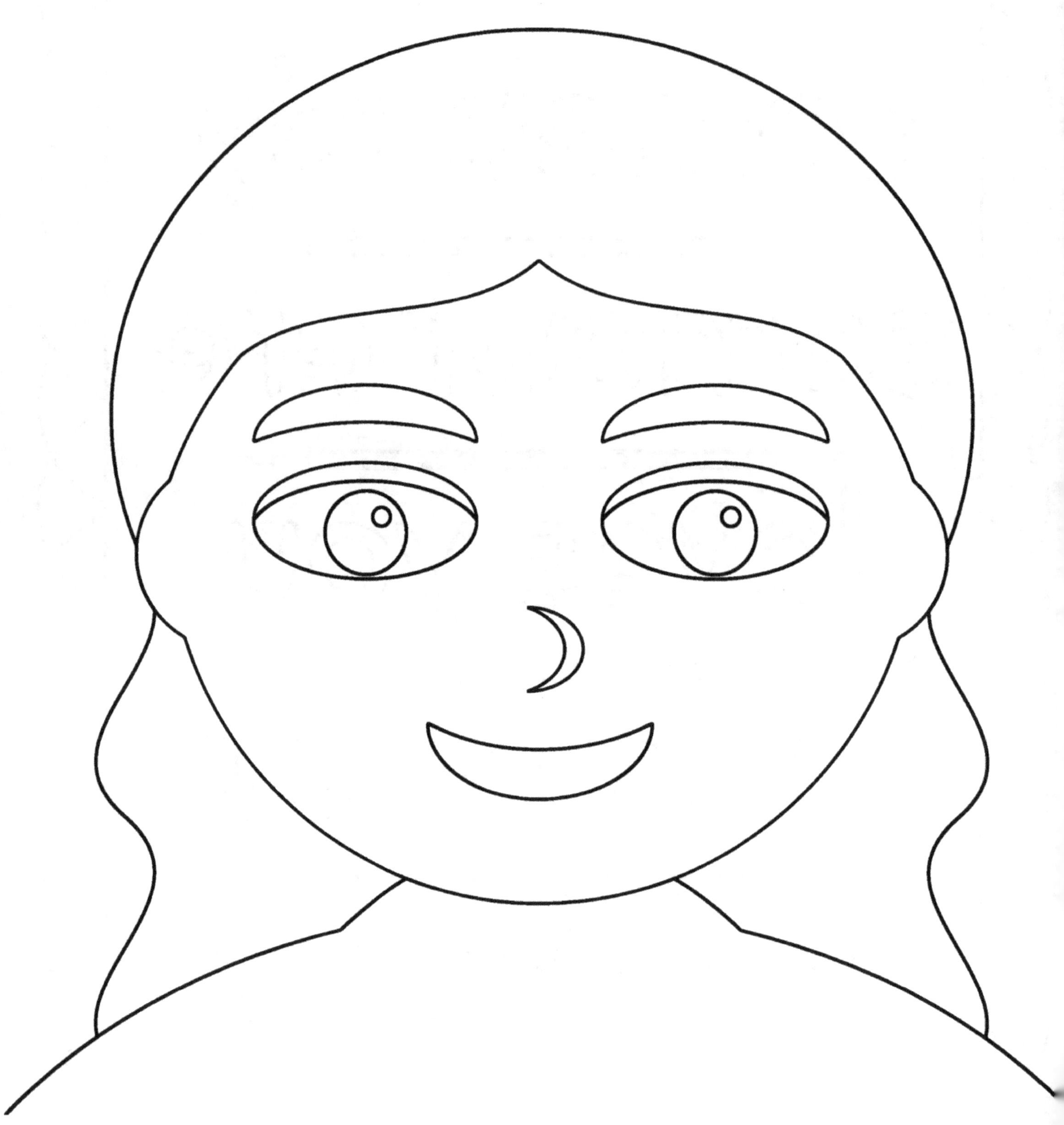

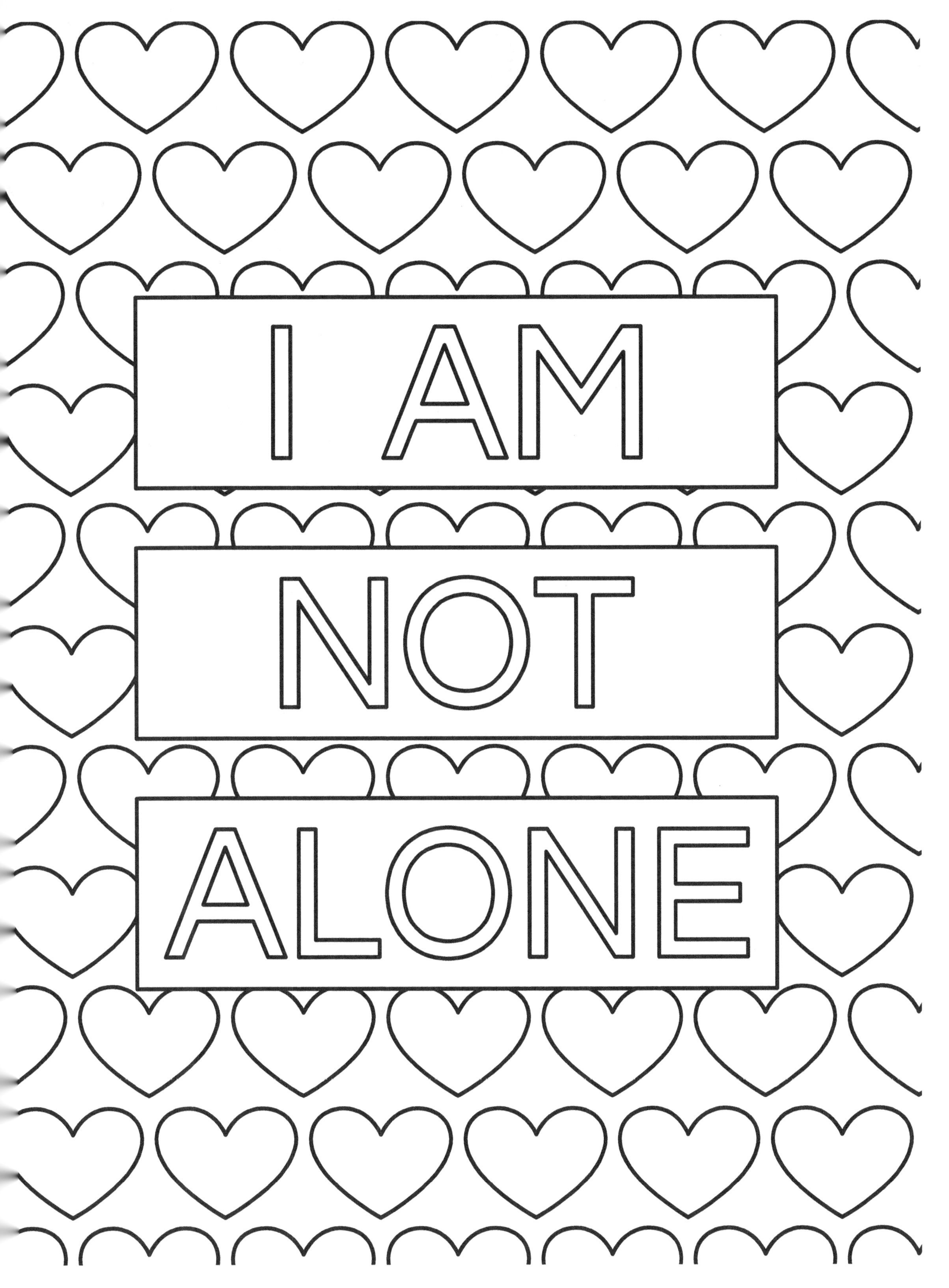

I AM
NOT
ALONE

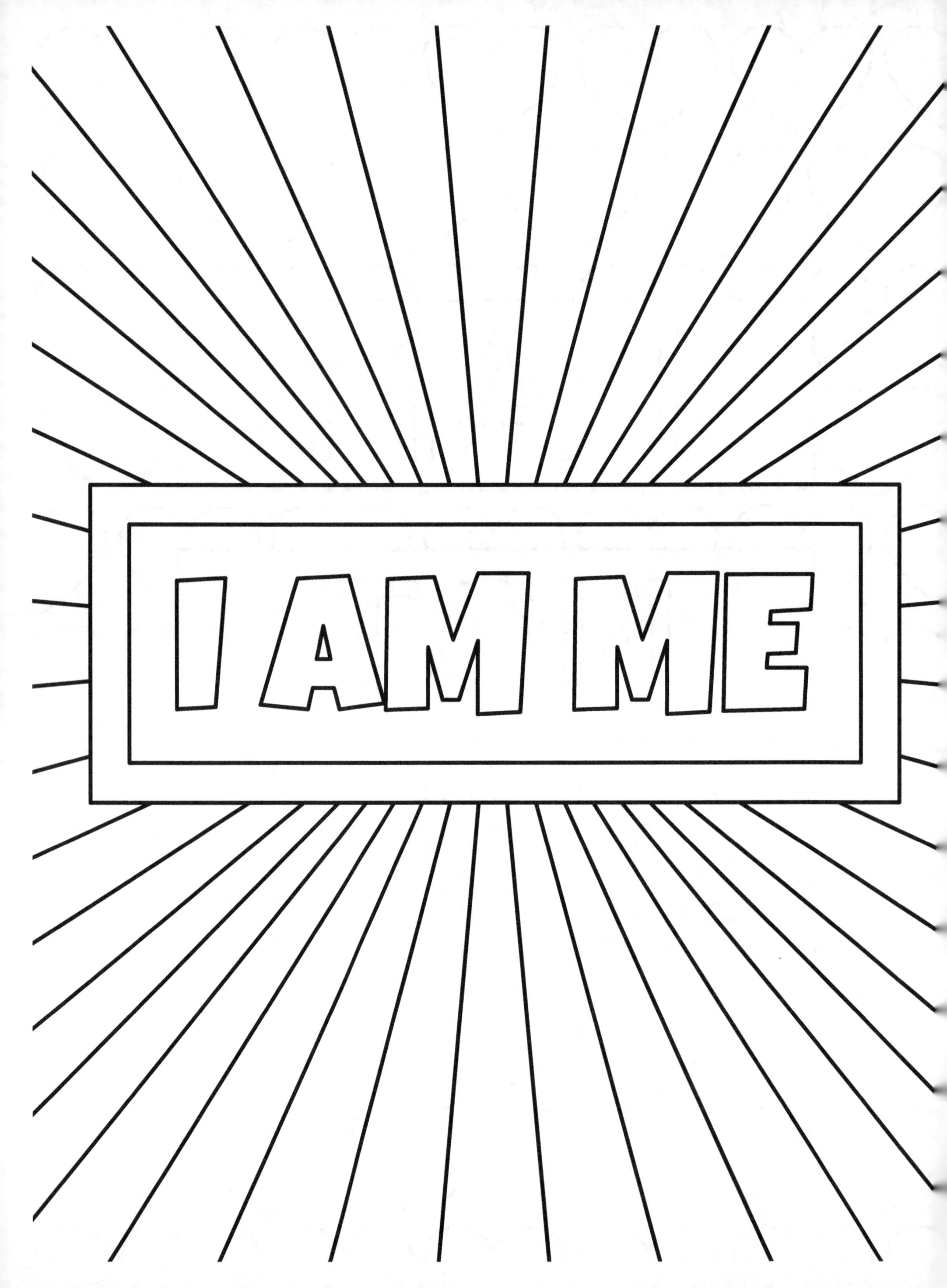

I AM ME

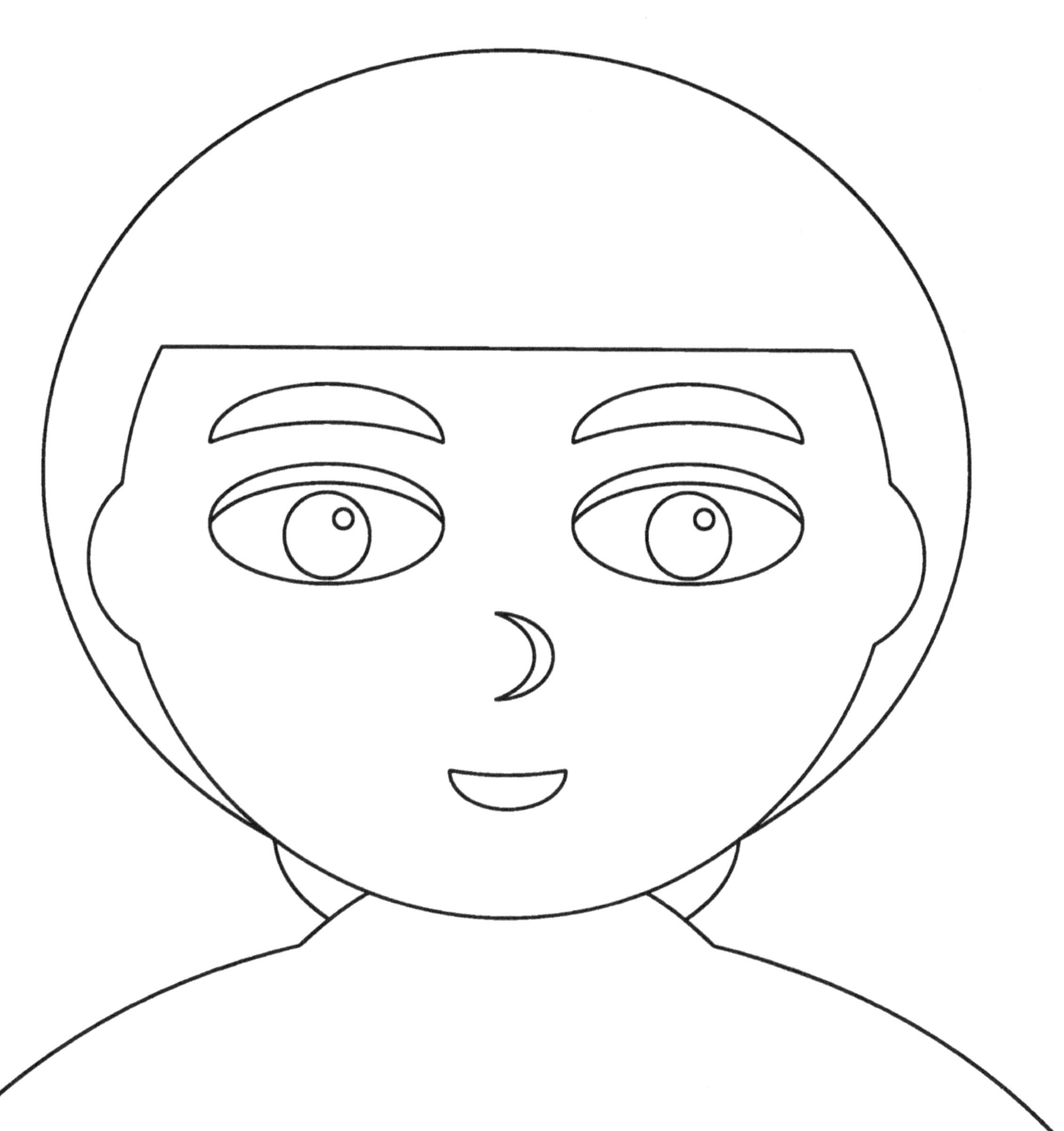

You were
never alone,
and you
never will be.

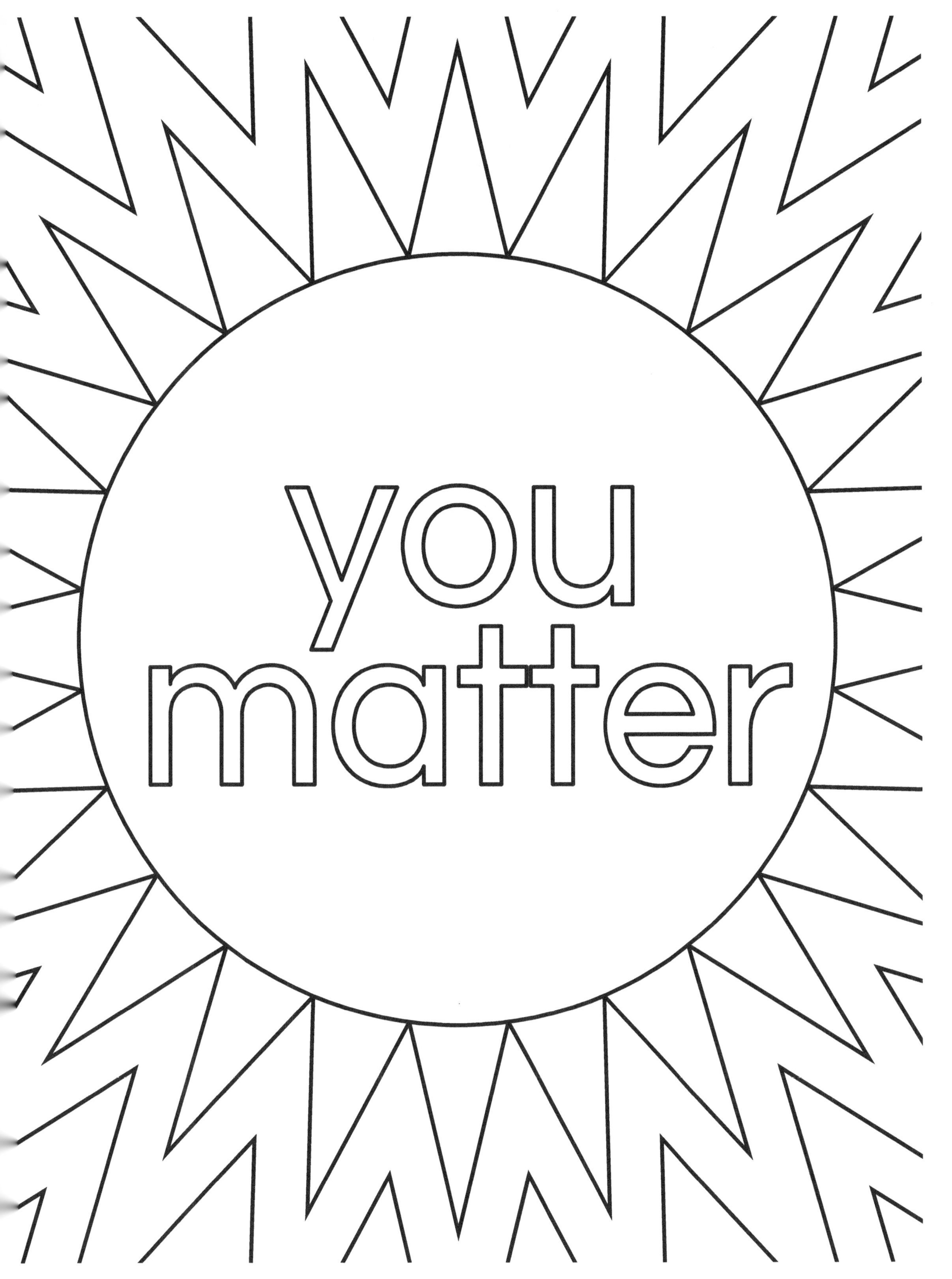

you
matter

MANY THANKS!

Dear Friend,

Thank you for choosing this coloring book! If you've enjoyed it, please don't forget to leave a review on Amazon, Goodreads, or wherever you're able to. Your positive review will help others find this book, too, and perhaps share it with others themselves. Even the shortest, most simple review makes a huge difference in helping spread the reach of this inclusive book, and more! Thank you so much for your support!